Growing People

INSTITUTE OF LEADERSHIP & MANAGEMENT (ILM)
THE PROFESSIONAL INSTITUTE OF CHOICE FOR TODAY'S MANAGER

Founded over 50 years ago and now part of the City & Guilds Group, the Institute of Leadership & Management (ILM) is unique among professional bodies. As the largest awarding body for management – related qualifications with over 75,000 candidates each year, the ILM recognises and fosters good management practice. As a professional body, ILM also offers informal personal and professional support to practising leaders and managers across all disciplines and at every career stage.

20,000 members have already found that ILM membership gives them the strategic, ongoing support they need to fulfil their aims, enabling them to enhance their skills, add to their professional expertise and to develop a wider network of valuable business contacts.

For further information on becoming a member of ILM please contact the Membership Department on telephone + 44 (0) 1543 251 346. www.i-l-m.com

Growing People

Learning and developing from day to day experience

BOB THOMSON

Chandos Publishing
Oxford · England

Published in association with

Institute of Leadership
& Management

Chandos Publishing (Oxford) Limited
Chandos House
5 & 6 Steadys Lane
Stanton Harcourt
Oxford OX29 5RL
UK
Tel: +44 (0) 1865 884447 Fax: +44 (0) 1865 884448
Email: info@chandospublishing.com
www.chandospublishing.com

First published in Great Britain in 2006

ISBN:
1 84334 213 8 (paperback)
1 84334 214 6 (hardback)
978 1 84334 213 7 (paperback)
978 1 84334 214 4 (hardback)

British Library Cataloguing-in-Publication Data.
A catalogue record for this book is available from the British Library.

Typeset by Domex e-Data Pvt. Ltd.
Printed in the UK and USA.

To Val
and
David, Eleanor, Dominic and Olivia

In reality, every reader is, while he is reading, the reader of his own self. The writer's work is merely a kind of optical instrument which he offers to the reader to enable him to discern what, without this book, he would perhaps never have experienced in himself. And the recognition by the reader in his own self of what the book says is the proof of its veracity.

Marcel Proust

Contents

List of figures   *xiii*

List of tables   *xv*

List of panels   *xvii*

Preface   *xix*

About the author   *xxiii*

1   Learning from experience   **1**

Introduction   1

What is learning?   2

On knowing   4

Transforming experience   6

Journalling   7

Going round the learning cycle   9

Learning styles   10

A strategy for developing people   12

The role of an off-job course   14

The environment created by top management   16

2   A coaching approach   **19**

Introduction   19

A conventional approach to managing people   19

A coaching approach to managing people   21

Coaching as a relationship   23

Control versus empowerment   25

Listening   28

Questioning 29

The GROW framework 31

The manager coach 35

Coaching and development reviews 38

3   Giving, generating and gathering feedback   41

Introduction 41

Giving feedback 42

Generating feedback 44

Feedforward 47

Gathering feedback 48

360-degree feedback 50

4   Mentoring   55

Introduction 55

What is mentoring? 55

Where mentoring is particularly useful 57

The benefits of being a mentor 59

What makes a good mentor? 60

The mentoring relationship 61

Guidelines for an internal mentoring scheme 62

Is the mentor a sponsor? 65

Alternatives to mentoring 66

5   Developing teams and organisations   71

Introduction 71

Coaching a team 71

What is a team? 74

Stages of team development 76

A team development exercise 78

A learning organisation 80

Organisational memory: storing and retrieving
knowledge   81

Creating a learning organisation or team:
a systematic approach   83

6   **Creating relationships**   **87**

Introduction   87

Images of organisation   88

Images of manager   91

Adult:adult relationships   93

Emotional intelligence   96

Developing your emotional intelligence   98

7   **Conversations that make a difference**   **101**

Introduction   101

From debate to dialogue   102

Listening   103

Inquiring   104

Ladder of inference   106

Voicing   107

Silence   110

Debate and dialogue   111

Difficult conversations   113

Tackling difficult conversations   115

Making sense of conversations   116

8   **Talent management**   **119**

Introduction   119

Overview of talent management   120

A model of leadership qualities and behaviours   124

Effective one-to-one development reviews   127

A talent review meeting   128

Feedback after a talent review   131

Information on people   133

An independent assessment process   135

Opportunities to gain new experiences   137

Finding non-executive opportunities   139

Processes to learn from these experiences   140

Key development investments   141

A talent management database   143

A critical roles model of succession management   144

The commitment of the chief executive   145

Bibliography   **147**

Index   *149*

List of figures

1.1 The learning cycle   2

1.2 The learning cycle (after David Kolb)   3

2.1 Cycle of control   26

2.2 Cycle of empowerment   27

2.3 Cycle of development   27

2.4 A development review form   39

5.1 The Coverdale systematic approach   84

6.1 Emotional intelligence   97

7.1 Iceberg diagram   104

7.2 Ladder of inference   107

7.3 David Kantor's four player model   118

8.1 The aim of talent management   120

8.2 What defines talent?   121

8.3 Who are your talented people?   122

8.4 How will you develop this talent?   124

8.5 A talent review form   130

8.6 A model of information (after Max Boisot)   133

List of tables

2.1 Closed and open questions   30

2.2 David Hemery's coaching dance   37

3.1 John Whitmore's five levels of feedback   46

7.1 Differences between debate and dialogue   111

7.2 Distinguishing blame from contribution   116

8.1 A set of leadership attributes   126

List of panels

2.1 Typical questions for a silent coaching session   33

3.1 Role analysis exercise   49

5.1 A team development exercise   78

7.1 Thinking rounds and validated listening   109

Preface

You cannot teach people anything. You can only help them to discover it within themselves. (Galileo)

I strongly believe that deep and sustained learning – that is, becoming able to do something you couldn't do before – only comes through experience. Experience on its own isn't enough, however. You need to reflect on and make sense of your experience to create knowledge, and this knowledge deepens when you apply it in new situations. This can be viewed as a learning cycle (see Figure 1.1, p. 2).

In this book I want to explore how you can use this notion of learning from experience to build the capability of those who work for you. People learn most from doing things they haven't done before. If you are looking to develop people, you need to offer them new experiences that they will find challenging but achievable. You also need to help them to reflect on and learn from these experiences.

This works at both an individual and team level. Your team will develop confidence and capability when it tackles fresh challenges and systematically reviews how it has performed.

If everyday experience is crucial, the implications for learning and development are profound. A learning and development strategy needs two key elements. First, it needs to offer real-time experiences to people. Second, it needs to offer processes to help them to review and learn from their experiences. While there is a place for off-job training programmes, you will develop people much more effectively by using processes such as coaching, mentoring and feedback to help them learn from their day-to-day activities. You may also save quite a bit of money from your training and development budget.

Chapter 1 looks in more detail at these notions of learning from experience and the learning cycle. This is the theory on which the practical chapters which make up the rest of the book are based.

Chapter 2 explores how as a manager you can adopt a coaching approach to help someone achieve high performance, develop their capability and realise their potential.

Chapter 3 considers the use of feedback as a catalyst to prompt someone to reflect on and learn from their experiences.

Chapter 4 looks at the use of experienced people within an organisation to act as mentors for younger employees. It also offers some guidelines to keep in mind when setting up a mentoring scheme within your organisation.

Chapter 5 moves the focus from helping individuals to considering how to use a coaching style of leadership with your team. We also explore what it means to be a learning organisation which systematically learns from its experience.

Chapter 6 invites you to reflect on the nature of the relationships which, as a manager, you inevitably have with each of the people who work for you. The nature of these relationships influences how effective you and your team are.

These relationships are fashioned day-by-day through the conversations you have – or fail to have – with people. Chapter 7 explores how you can create conversations that get to the heart of the matter and make a difference.

In the final chapter we consider how you and your colleagues on a management team can set up a talent management process to collectively identify and nurture the talented people within your organisation or department.

There are a number of people and experiences that have helped me on my own development journey and influenced the thinking behind this book. The foundation of my practice in management development was laid when I took part in the MA in Management Learning at Lancaster University. I have also benefited greatly from taking a Certificate in Counselling at Manchester University and a Certificate in Coaching at the School of Coaching. I would like to thank the faculty and fellow participants on these programmes.

My interest in experiential learning really began when I attended a one-week programme run for ICI by the Coverdale Organisation. This was a wonderful experience, and 25 years later I am still a huge fan of Coverdale, as you may gather from reading Chapter 5.

I took my first steps into the management development field while working as an economist in ICI's Mond Division in Runcorn, Cheshire. I am grateful to my manager at that time, Brian Luker, and Robin Eades and his training and development colleagues for enabling me to gain these early experiences of development work.

I left ICI to join the British Gas Management Centre near Stratford upon Avon, and spent seven happy years there learning my trade as I worked on management and graduate development programmes. Thanks to Phil Besley, Dave Cranage and all my other colleagues from those days.

When British Gas went through one of its many reorganisations in the mid-1990s I moved into a more strategic management development role in Transco. I worked alongside some great people there, and would like to thank Sean Murphy, Jim Borritt, Thea Mills, Will Large, Sara Abbott, Keith Hutchison, Maggie Matthews, Nicola Partridge, Emma Earnshaw, Catherine Hamilton, Pam Mosedale, Steve

Edgeworth, Adrian Duckett, Tina Smith and others for their friendship and support.

At Transco and later at National Grid Transco, I had the good fortune to commission management development programmes from – and work alongside – some superb organisations. The influence of John Whitmore, David Hemery, David Whitaker and Sue Slocombe of Performance Consultants is evident in the chapters on coaching and feedback. I learnt a lot about conversations from Gina Hayden of Sphere Consulting. My thinking on talent management and on 360-degree feedback owes much to the ideas of Andrew Munro of AM Ltd. I have also enjoyed and benefited from various collaborations with Nick Cowley and his colleagues associated with the Oxford Group.

Thanks too to Sue Godfrey, Jenny Summerfield, Dave Heddle, Charles Brook, Madeline McGill, Vicki Espin, Steve Briault, Robin Linnecar, Steve Schneider and other coaches and management development consultants for many stimulating conversations over the years.

You will see in the various quotes throughout the text and in the bibliography at the end of the book that I am indebted to a number of other people whose writings have influenced my approach to learning and development.

Thank you to Sue Lomas for putting me in touch with the publisher, to Dr Glyn Jones of Chandos Publishing (Oxford) Ltd. for his support and encouragement, and to Neill Johnstone for transforming my text into the final product.

Finally, I dedicate this book with love to my wife, Val, and our children, David, Eleanor, Dominic and Olivia, who give me the greatest learning experiences of my life – and much more besides.

About the author

Bob Thomson has worked in management development since 1988. He is currently the Management Development Adviser at the University of Warwick, and was previously Leadership Development Manager at National Grid Transco.

Before moving into management development he worked as an economist for eleven years with British Steel and ICI.

Bob has degrees in Maths, in Economics and in Management Learning. He also has qualifications and experience in Counselling and in Coaching.

He is married with four children and lives in Stratford upon Avon.

The author may be contacted at:

E-mail: *bob.thomson@warwick.ac.uk*

Learning from experience

There is nothing more practical than a good theory.
(Kurt Lewin)

Introduction

In this chapter I shall set out briefly the theory that
underpins my approach to developing people. This is the
theory on which the practical chapters which make up the
rest of the book are based.

Over 20 years ago, when I was learning to be a counsellor,
I read a sentence that profoundly affects how I think about
helping people to learn and develop. It is a sentence whose
meaning and implications I am still thinking about more
than two decades later. In *On Becoming a Person*, Carl
Rogers writes, 'It seems to me that anything that can be
taught to another is relatively inconsequential, and has little
or no influence on behavior.'

Some years later, around 1990, I had begun working in
management development at British Gas and was taking an
MA in Management Learning at Lancaster University. I read
David Kolb's book *Experiential Learning,* and the ideas set
out there gave me a theoretical foundation for my approach
to learning and development. In the next few pages I shall
set out a summary of what I took from Kolb's book.

What is learning?

In everyday use, learning is equated with taking in information. However, the kind of learning that I want to explore in this book is what Peter Senge calls 'real learning'. He writes, 'Through learning we become able to do something we never were able to do' (Senge, 1990). It is this kind of learning – becoming able to do new things – that you are looking to develop in those who work for you.

Deep and sustained learning – becoming able to do something you couldn't do before – only comes through experience.

Experience on its own, however, is not enough. Experience needs to be reflected upon and made sense of to create knowledge, and this knowledge deepens when it is applied in fresh situations. The process can be viewed as a learning cycle (Figure 1.1).

This learning cycle is my rewording in simpler language of the learning cycle set out by Kolb (1984). Figure 1.2 shows how he presents the learning cycle in his own terms.

To appreciate this, pause for a moment and consider how you learnt to drive a car (or something else you do well, if

Figure 1.1   The learning cycle

Experience

Performing differently

Reflection

Making sense of

Kolb, David A., EXPERIENTIAL LEARNING: Experience as the Source of Learning, (c) 1984. Adapted with the permission of Pearson Education, Inc, Upper Saddle River, NJ.

Figure 1.2 The learning cycle (after David Kolb)

Concrete experience

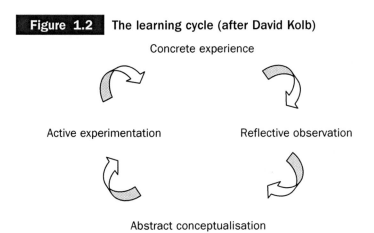

Active experimentation   Reflective observation

Abstract conceptualisation

you can't drive a car). Learning to drive requires lots of concrete experience, which in this context means time spent behind the wheel. When you are learning to drive you will think about things that happened when you were behind the wheel, particularly if you make a mistake. In other words, you will reflect on your experience. You can't learn to drive a car simply by reading a book or attending a lecture. You do, however, need some 'concepts', such as, *this is what the accelerator, brake and clutch pedals do.* And, as your skill level develops, you will begin to drive differently – for example, checking your rear-view mirror more or less frequently than when you were a novice.

The 'south pole' of the learning cycle – what I have called *making sense of* and what Kolb calls *abstract conceptualisation* – is sometimes referred to as *theory.* There are two types of theory that may come into play here. The first is someone else's theory, which may be offered in a lecture or a book. The second kind of theory is one that you create for yourself. This may be prompted by someone else's theory which you refine and internalise for yourself. For example, I am setting out here my version of the learning cycle where the language means more to me than the original learning cycle of

Kolb. The theory which you devise yourself or which you refine from someone else's will be more meaningful for you.

Kurt Lewin writes that 'There is nothing more practical than a good theory'. As a management development professional, I continually use Kolb's theory of the learning cycle – or my adaptation of it – as the basis of my practice.

Kolb offers the following definition of learning which is the basis of the approach to developing people that will be explored in this book: 'Learning is the process whereby knowledge is created through the transformation of experience'.

Since this notion of learning from experience is fundamental to everything that follows, I want to spend a little time exploring some aspects of the learning cycle. If you are an action-oriented manager, then you might want to skip this and jump to the later chapters which translate the theory into practical ways of helping your people to reflect upon and learn from their day-to-day experiences.

On knowing

Many languages have two words for the verb *to know*. For example, French has *connaître* and *savoir* while German has *kennen* and *wissen*.

Kolb argues that there are two ways of knowing the world, *apprehension* and *comprehension*. Thus, to say that I know a person (*connaître, kennen...*) is different from saying that I know mathematics (*savoir, wissen...*) The first way of knowing involves (in Kolb's terminology) concrete experience, while the latter involves abstract conceptualisation.

The English language, however, uses the same verb, *to know*, in both senses. Kolb illustrates the difference with a quote from Shakespeare's *A Midsummer Night's Dream*:

> Lovers and madmen have such seething brains,
> Such shaping fantasies, that apprehend
> More than cool reason even comprehends.

Kolb argues that these two ways of knowing the world are 'distinct' and 'coequal', He characterises the two different ways of knowing in the following pairs:

concrete experience	abstract conceptualisation
connaître, kennen	*savoir, wissen*
apprehension	comprehension
knowledge of – acquaintance	knowledge about
feelings	thoughts
concrete	abstract
appreciation	criticism
personal knowledge	social knowledge

Kolb also argues that, 'the dynamic relation between comprehension and apprehension lies at the core of knowledge creation'.

This is a very important point. We need both theory and experience to create knowledge. Moreover, theory and experience interact dynamically. Kolb illustrates this with a quote from Einstein:

> I see on the one side the totality of sense experiences and, on the other, the totality of concepts and propositions which are laid down in books ... The concepts and propositions get 'meaning', viz. 'content' only through their connection with sense-experiences. The connection of the latter with the former is purely intuitive, not itself of a logical nature. The degree of certainty with which this relation, viz. intuitive connection, can be undertaken, and nothing else differentiates empty phantasy from scientific 'truth'.

Thus, the creation of knowledge – the development of managerial capability as well as the process of scientific discovery – requires a dynamic interaction between the concrete and the abstract, between our feelings and our thoughts. I wonder if you have ever had one of those 'aha!' moments when you hear or read something and some past experiences click into place and you make sense of things. That is an example of the dynamic interaction between theory and experience.

Transforming experience

The north-south dimension of the Kolb learning cycle represents how we take hold of – or *grasp* – our experience. The east-west dimension represents how we *transform* this grasp. Kolb writes:

> Knowledge results from the combination of grasping experience and transforming it.
>
> The central idea here is that learning, and therefore knowing, requires both a grasp or figurative representation of experience and some transformation of that representation. (Kolb, 1984)

In other words, we need to transform our experience by either reflecting upon it or by doing something with it.

In the words of Aldous Huxley, 'Experience is not what happens to you. It is what you do with what happens to you'.

When I run a workshop I usually invite each participant near the close to identify what he or she is going to do differently. Some people may not at that point be ready to commit to action, which is fine, but I am keen to encourage people to do something with whatever they have learnt at the workshop. At the end of the workshop, when I hear the feedback '*that was interesting*', I feel disappointed because *interesting* is not enough – to make a difference it has to be *useful*. I am hoping that the participants will do something with whatever they have – in Kolb's term – grasped.

While doing something differently is obviously an active process, it does not follow that reflecting is a passive activity. In *Reflection: Turning Experience into Learning*, David Boud, Rosemary Keogh and David Walker point out that:

> Reflection ... is an active process of exploration and discovery, which often leads to very unexpected outcomes.
> Reflection ... is pursued with intent. It is not idle meanderings or day-dreaming, but purposive activity directed towards a goal. (Boud et al., 1985)

The importance of experience coupled with reflection as the basis for developing managers is captured by Henry Mintzberg in his book *Managers Not MBAs*:

> The key ingredient for management education is natural experience that has been lived in everyday life, on the job and off ... The most powerful learning comes from reflecting on experiences that have been lived naturally. Indeed, because every practicing manager is loaded with such experiences, a classroom full of such managers makes for a most remarkable learning situation. (Mintzberg, 2004)

Journalling

One very simple and inexpensive way of reflecting on your experience is to keep a journal. By a journal I don't mean a diary which records events. Rather, a journal is a place where you can record important experiences, how you responded, and your thoughts and feelings about what happened. It is a place where you can take some private time to explore what is going on for you. It is also a place where you can look forwards and explore your hopes and plans for the future.

Madeline McGill writes:

> A journal is a place where we can be ourselves – where we do not have to pose – where we can remember and reflect on significant thoughts and events and so re-integrate them into the panorama of life...
>
> It is a means of talking and listening to ourselves – a way of 'speaking our thoughts' – of having a dialogue with ourselves...

A journal is clearly a very personal thing, and keeping a journal will not appeal to everyone. There is no one style or format – you will find the style of journal that works for you. It may be in a notebook or on a personal computer. It may contain drawings or quotations or pieces of poetry. It is not a work of literature, and you don't need to record your thoughts in perfect prose.

One way of working with a journal is to capture some headlines – a summary of what happened and how you felt – and then, when you are ready and have more time, to reflect more closely on what lies behind the headlines.

Reflecting on what happened and your thoughts and feelings will help you to learn from an experience. Over time patterns may emerge, and you understand more deeply the meaning of events and appreciate more clearly your own motives and feelings and behaviour. For example, on re-reading your journal you might find that several times in the last year you have been in the same kind of confrontational situation and on each occasion you responded by withdrawing. Reflecting on this might lead to a deeper level of learning and commitment to action.

A journal can be particularly useful when you are going through a period of change or when you are at a crossroads facing an importance decision. It can also give you a sense of progress – or perhaps stagnation.

Going round the learning cycle

At the beginning of the chapter we described the process of learning from experience as a learning cycle that you need to go round in order to learn effectively. You can begin this process at any one of the four points of the learning cycle. For example:

- *Theory*: You read a cookery book and decide to try out a new recipe.

- *Experimentation*: Some friends arrive unexpectedly and you cook up whatever you can find in the fridge to make a new and surprisingly tasty risotto.

- *Experience*: At dinner at a friend's house you eat something delicious and ask for the recipe.

- *Reflection*: You start a diet and consider how you can make some of your favourite dishes using alternative low calorie ingredients.

The learning cycle is actually a learning spiral which you can go round many times with increasing expertise and fluency. You learn to drive, for example, through a series of lessons, not just one. And once you have passed your test, you can still improve considerably as you gain further experience or as you apply what you learn from an advanced driving course.

You can go round the learning cycle in seconds – something happens, you pause, something clicks, and you adjust your approach – or you can spend a lifetime blocked at some point and, therefore, not learning. For example, I am hopeless at DIY, and will never get any better unless I take a risk and begin to experiment by, say, putting up some shelves.

Learning styles

Kolb's view that there are two ways of grasping experience and two ways of transforming it leads to the idea of four different learning styles.

Peter Honey and Alan Mumford have a variation of the learning cycle which suggests that people have a preference for one of the following four learning styles:

- *Activists*: who involve themselves fully and without bias in new learning experiences.
- *Reflectors*: who like to stand back and ponder experiences and observe them from many different perspectives.
- *Theorists*: who adapt and integrate observations into complex but logically sound theories.
- *Pragmatists*: who are keen to try out ideas, theories and techniques to see if they work in practice. (Honey and Mumford, 2000)

These notions of learning styles are widely used – for example, a good learning design is supposed to have activities that appeal to all four learning styles.

I am not convinced that people do have individual learning styles. My view is that people have preferences on how they like to spend their time. For example, most engineers like to be active doing things and dislike spending time reflecting or exploring their feelings. This does not mean, however, that this is how they learn. Rather, it is simply what they enjoy more.

I think that the nature of what you are trying to learn matters more than how you prefer to spend your time. To learn philosophy requires a lot of reflection. To learn how to swim you will need to get in the water. To learn how to counsel requires that you be aware of your own and others' feelings. To become a mathematician requires the ability to understand abstract theories.

To be really good at something requires you to spend time at all four points of the learning cycle. A Nobel Prize winning scientist will appreciate the beauty as well as the logic of science. A top-class mountaineer will not only scale new heights but will also review his expeditions to draw the lessons for next time.

As an illustration of the importance of being able to engage effectively at all points of the learning cycle, consider the following description of Erwin Rommel, the outstanding German commander of the Second World War. In his biography of Rommel, *Knight's Cross*, David Fraser describes a supreme man of action who also reflected deeply on his experiences of battle, made sense of them and communicated his sense to others:

> He leapt at every experience of battle, but he turned experience into military wisdom by his shrewdness and his objectivity. There thus emerged not only a superb man of action but a military philosopher. It was this gift of Rommel's for distilling experience, for translating individual achievement, recollected, into the

language of enduring – and universal – operational and tactical lessons which made him remarkable and lay at the heart of his success. He could, throughout life, decide fast, act boldly, remember clearly, narrate vividly, ponder and deduce wisely. (Fraser, 1993)

A strategy for developing people

My basic proposition is that real learning – becoming able to do new things – requires real experience coupled with reflection to make sense of that experience. If this is indeed how people learn how to do new things, then the implications for learning and development are profound. A learning and development strategy needs two key elements. First, it needs to offer real-time experiences to people. Second, it needs to offer processes to help them to review and learn from their experiences. These themes will be developed in the remainder of the book.

In a similar way, you as a manager who wants to build the capability of your people need, first, to offer them challenging experiences and, second, to help them to learn from these experiences. Moreover, you will find that such an approach is not only more effective at developing people but also is far less expensive than traditional approaches based on courses and programmes.

In your own situation you know what tasks and projects have to be done by your team. You also have some sense of who in your team can do these well. One of your challenges is to balance giving work to someone who can already do it with asking someone to take it on because it will stretch and develop them. You may have to make a trade-off between short-term delivery of results against longer-term development of capability. In some instances you may want to ask several people to become involved, perhaps bringing together a blend of youth and experience. You will know what is possible and acceptable in your own work environment. I encourage you to think explicitly about this when you allocate work or put together a project team.

In *High Flyers* Morgan McCall writes, 'The principle is simple: people learn most by doing things they haven't done before'. He goes on to say that because experiences are happening all the time and assignments are being filled somehow by someone, development is, in a sense, a sunk cost for an organisation. Development then 'is about using what happens in a wiser manner' (McCall, 1998).

In a similar fashion, Tim Gallwey in *The Inner Game of Work* recommends a seminar that:

- takes very little extra time and no extra money;
- is the best seminar ever designed;
- is highly interactive and has incredible three-dimensional graphics;
- will teach you exactly what you most need to learn.

This seminar is your everyday life. To gain admission, he writes, 'You must declare yourself to be a *learner* during your working hours as well as a doer' (Gallwey, 2000).

At the beginning of the chapter I quoted some words of Carl Rogers that have profoundly influenced my approach to management development, coaching and counselling: 'It seems to me that anything that can be taught to another is relatively inconsequential, and has little or no influence on behavior'. This statement echoes some words of Galileo: 'You cannot teach people anything. You can only help them to discover it within themselves'.

Taken together, the various quotes in this section pose a major challenge to traditional approaches to development which involve simply sending people on courses. Publishing a menu of courses, delivered in-house or externally, offers some reassurance to organisations that they are looking after the development of their people. This reassurance can also be quantified in terms of either money or trainee days. However, I suggest that this reassurance is an illusion. Developing people is much more about what happens on the job and more generally in daily life than about attending courses. It is, to repeat, about creating opportunities for people to do new things and then helping them to learn from these opportunities.

The role of an off-job course

Having questioned the value of off-job courses and programmes, I am not, however, saying that they have no part to play in a coherent strategy for learning and development. So, if real-time experience is vital, what is the role of an off-job event in developing people?

One way of looking at this is to recognise that participation in a workshop offers the opportunity to engage at all four points of the learning cycle. When I design a learning event – an individual exercise, a two-day course or a twelve-month programme – I use the notion of the learning cycle as the framework and try to build in elements of experience, reflection, theory and action planning.

- *Experience*: A workshop can be used to simulate an experience that might be too costly or risky to under-take for real. For example, a business game lets inexperienced managers make financial decisions and see the effects without risking the success of the real business.

- *Reflection*: Managers are extremely busy these days, often caught up in day-to-day activities with seemingly little time to stand back. Taking a couple of days out gives them the opportunity to reflect and make sense of their experience. It also gives them the chance to network with their peers and to hear how they have tackled issues.

- *Theory*: Participation on a workshop offers managers the chance to listen to and understand theories and models, or to create their own frameworks that make sense of their world.

- *Experimentation*: A workshop on, for example, presentation skills or assertiveness gives people the chance to practise new skills or behaviours in relative safety, enabling them to make mistakes and learn from them. It can also give them the chance to make action plans about what they will do differently back at work as a result of their learning.

The value of these different stances coming together is summarised by Henry Mintzberg:

> The purpose of getting people together for development is neither to fill them full of concepts nor to provide them with the opportunity to talk; it is to stimulate learning at the interface of these two: where concepts, seriously presented, meet experiences, deeply lived. (Mintzberg, 2004)

Although the place for off-job courses is often exaggerated in both the time and money spent, my view is that they can be useful if they are focused carefully on key needs and if they are designed to embrace the various aspects of the learning cycle.

The environment created by top management

I said previously that the two key elements in a learning and development strategy are real-time experiences coupled with processes to review and learn from experience. There is, however, a third element which will determine how successful the strategy is – the commitment from the top of the organisation, especially the commitment of the person at the very top.

The commitment you need is through actions not merely words. It is easy for a chief executive to say that developing people is important – *Our people are our greatest asset*. But this needs to be backed up by the appropriate investment in resources and by the example set from the top.

Morgan McCall observes that, if you want bees to make honey you need to create the right environment around the hive, not issue protocols about carbohydrate chemistry. He argues that, if senior managers do not develop themselves and help develop others, 'then even the most elegant development 'system' will be little more than an exercise'.

There is a chapter in *The Fifth Discipline* called 'A Manager's Time' where Peter Senge asks, 'How can we expect people to learn when they have little time to think and reflect, individually and collaboratively?' He questions whether the 'incessant busyness' which is a feature of modern management is an effective way of working. He goes on to write that, 'The management of time and attention is an area where top management has a significant influence, not by edict but by example'.

His vision of managerial work in a learning organisation is one where 'Action will still be critical, but incisive action will not be confused with incessant activity. There will be time for reflection, conceptualising, and examining complex issues'.

It is vital that those at the top of the organisation – through their actions – set an example which encourages managers to reflect, to conceptualise, to coach, to give feedback, and to develop both themselves and those who work for them.

As McCall comments, 'Above all, the development of leadership is a leadership issue'.

A coaching approach

If your employees believe their job is to do what you tell them, you're sunk. (Susan Scott)

Introduction

In this chapter I describe a coaching approach to managing and developing people. I hope to show that using a coaching style will help you achieve high performance from your people and also build their capability over time. A coaching style of management can enable you to offer your people challenging experiences at the edge of their comfort zone, which is where learning takes place. It can also assist you in helping your people to reflect on and learn from these experiences.

Before looking at coaching, however, let us begin by considering a more conventional approach to management.

A conventional approach to managing people

A manager, by definition, is someone who achieves results through other people rather than exclusively through their own efforts. So, how does a manager go about achieving results through others?

A conventional answer is that the manager sets objectives for their people, communicates them clearly and monitors the achievement of these objectives. In many cases the objectives arise as a result of higher-level business objectives which cascade down the organisation. *Management by objectives* is a rational, clear approach to achieving results. In many organisations this is crystallised in an annual performance management cycle based on performance reviews which measure how well last year's objectives were achieved and which set the objectives for the coming year.

In setting and monitoring objectives for your staff, you in effect *tell* your people what to do. This *telling* approach is very much the norm – generally an unspoken and unconscious norm – in many organisations. Managers are expected to know what is going on and to tell people what to do. Often the people being managed in this way expect this at least as strongly as those in authority.

There are a number of advantages in a telling approach. Telling is quicker, certainly in the short run. Senior people often know more of the bigger picture and so can make more informed decisions about what is required. Sometimes it is obvious what needs to be done and it is entirely appropriate simply to say so. In an emergency or a crisis, a clear command is extremely useful.

Telling is sometimes described in a disapproving way as *command and control*. Indeed, later in the chapter I shall be critical of an overemphasis on telling. Putting this in more neutral language, telling is about giving instructions, ensuring that these instructions are carried out and restricting the scope for discretion and judgment. There are many situations in which this is appropriate. When I'm depositing a cheque at a bank, receiving a blood transfusion in a hospital or having my car brakes repaired in a garage, I want there to be well-defined procedures that staff carry out consistently.

Nonetheless, there are downsides in a management style which is exclusively telling. If you only ever tell your people what to do, then you don't tap into their experience, their knowledge of what is really going on, and their ideas about how to do things better. You run the risk of getting compliance but no real commitment or sense of ownership. When things go wrong, people will look to you for the answer rather than use their initiative. Continually telling can be very time consuming and, as you don't develop your people, you need to keep on spending your time telling them what to do.

As a simple illustration, imagine that you have a four-year-old son whose shoe laces need tying. It will be quicker today to tie them for him. However, if you are still tying his shoe laces ten years later, you will have wasted an awful lot of time and effort. Showing him how to tie his shoelaces – a small act of empowerment, if you like – makes him more independent and in the long run saves you lots of time.

A coaching approach to managing people

In everyday language we think of a coach – often a sports coach – as someone who knows better than the players how the game should be played, who will tell the players the tactics to be followed, and who understands all the techniques even though they may not be as talented as the players being coached. This is *not* what I mean by coaching in this book. In saying that, I am not criticising the sports coach, merely clarifying my terms.

It is very simple to state the essence of the type of coaching that I want to explore in this chapter. When coaching someone you are trying to do two things – to raise the individual's awareness and to help the individual to take responsibility for their actions. It is as straightforward as that. Someone who is aware of what needs to be done and how to do it, and who takes responsibility for doing it, will perform effectively.

This can be thought of as an equation:

Awareness + Responsibility = Performance

(John Whitmore, however, says that awareness *without* responsibility is just whingeing.)

Moreover, there are two basic skills which you need to coach successfully. First, you must be able to listen well and, second, you must be able to ask effective questions. Your challenge as a manager is simply to listen and ask questions which raise awareness and encourage responsibility in the performer.

This is deceptively easy to state and hard to put into practice. It is a bit like playing chess. It might take half an hour to learn all the rules and moves but a lifetime to become a grandmaster.

There are a variety of definitions of coaching. The one that I prefer is:

> Coaching is a relationship to facilitate the performance, learning or development of another.

The Change Partnership, a leading executive coaching firm, describe what happens in a productive coaching relationship in their brochure *What is Coaching?*

> The essence of Coaching is that the individual being coached thinks through their situation, creates a strategy

for improvement, prepares and then implements plans to achieve it, and reviews progress and outcomes with the Coach to ensure that the maximum learning – the best possible experience – is wrung from the process.

This view of coaching is set out very clearly by John Whitmore in his book *Coaching for Performance*. He writes that, 'Coaching is unlocking a person's potential to maximise their own performance. It is helping them to learn rather than teaching them' (Whitmore, 2002).

Coaches can operate along a spectrum from non-directive to directive, and many coaches will move along this spectrum depending on the needs of the individual. We shall see that there is a place for telling people what to do within a coaching approach, but that this is limited. It is undoubtedly quicker and easier when the coach operates more closely to the directive end of the spectrum and offers suggestions. And this is often what the individual is looking for from the coach.

My own preference in coaching, however, is to be close to the non-directive end. This is where real learning, change and growth become possible. In my view, when as a manager you coach your people effectively you will primarily be using a non-directive approach to tap into their experience and ideas.

Coaching as a relationship

The above definition of coaching emphasises that coaching is a relationship. In a later chapter we consider in more detail different ways of viewing the relationship you as a manager have with your people. For now, however, I want to emphasise that the differences between a *command and control* approach and a *coaching* approach to managing people are profound. Command and control is based on hierarchical relationships. The manager knows best and the individual needs some judicious combination of praise or criticism to perform. Coaching is based on egalitarian relationships. Both parties have key information, and the individual needs a blend of support and challenge to perform – and develop.

How you view the people who work for you is crucial. A coaching approach calls for a genuine belief in the potential of people, a trust that others will perform, and a willingness to let go and see what happens. These are tough requirements. My own view is that only a coaching approach which taps into the potential, creativity and integrity of others will deliver outstanding performance. Moreover, coaching that delivers outstanding performance cannot fail – at the same time – to grow the capability of people.

Many managers – brought up in organisations where command and control was the norm – will find these requirements scary, naïve, idealistic or simply impractical. They will dismiss a coaching approach. And so they will go on getting the results they have been getting by telling people what to do and monitoring carefully. Sometimes these results will be excellent but they will never be transformational. For, as Meg Wheatley writes, 'When obedience and compliance are the primary values, then creativity, commitment and generosity are destroyed' (Wheatley, 2002).

I have encountered some managers with a compulsive need to know everything that is going on and to feel that they are making or at least approving every decision. While they may achieve reasonable results, they inevitably work long hours and create a culture of dependency, risk aversion and often fear. Moreover, their people resent this micro-management, and morale in a department led by an over-controlling manager is often dreadful. Morgan McCall underlines these points when he writes:

> Among other things, overmanagers can be guilty of meddling in things they don't understand, alienating the people whose help they need, making a lot of mistakes because they don't listen to experts or because the experts don't care to help them, or getting mired in details and not thinking broadly. Some micromanagers get so busy doing everyone else's job that they don't do their own. (McCall, 1998)

If you establish a coaching style of management and avoid getting immersed in detail, then not only will your people perform and develop but you will also free your own time to think more strategically and to work fewer hours.

Control versus empowerment

The following figures are another way of illustrating the different possible outcomes when you adopt a coaching approach to managing your people, as opposed to a controlling approach. First, consider the effect on someone who works for a manager who is heavily into control with a dominant *tell* style. Constantly told what to do, the individual doesn't need to think particularly hard. Their awareness isn't raised and they do not take responsibility beyond doing what they are told. Their view of their ability is more limited than it might have been as they are simply someone who carries out instructions. With all these constraints, they will be looking to be told what to do next time too. Figure 2.1 illustrates this as a cycle of control.

Figure 2.1 Cycle of control

Coach tells more

Performer has less self-belief

Performer thinks less

Performer takes less responsibility

Performer less aware

On the other hand, consider someone who works for a manager with a coaching style. Skilful questions prompt the individual to think more deeply or carefully about what they are doing. They become more aware of what is required and take more responsibility for delivering what the organisation needs. They believe they are a capable performer who is making a useful contribution. They expect to bring their own ideas and strengths to the next task in hand. In other words, the organisation uses more of their potential, they make a greater contribution, and they feel more satisfied in their role. Figure 2.2 illustrates this as a cycle of empowerment.

Note that there are both short- and long-term effects here. In the short term, telling means that the individual brings less of their ability to the task whereas coaching will engage more of their skills and ideas. Since we learn through experience, capability grows when someone is coached. The individual's view of themselves and what they can contribute grow too. They begin to aim higher and in the long run

Figure 2.2 Cycle of empowerment

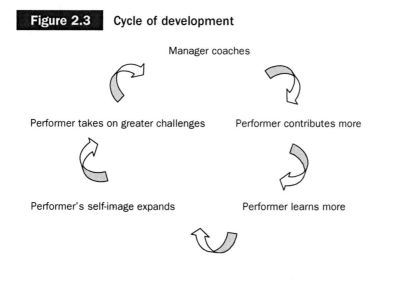

Coach listens and asks open questions

Performer has more self-belief

Performer thinks more

Performer takes more responsibility

Performer more aware

become a more capable performer who can take on bigger tasks and roles. In other words, coaching not only produces higher performance, it also builds future capability. Figure 2.3 illustrates this as a cycle of development.

This is like the recurrent pattern found by John Kotter among successful general managers, which he calls the *success syndrome*. He writes of these managers that:

Figure 2.3 Cycle of development

Manager coaches

Performer takes on greater challenges

Performer contributes more

Performer's self-image expands

Performer learns more

They did well in an early assignment; that led to a promotion, or a somewhat more challenging assignment; that reinforced (or even increased) their self-esteem and motivation and led to an increase in their formal or informal power and an increase in the opportunities available to develop more power. More challenging jobs also stretched them and helped build their skills. (Kotter, 1982)

Listening

We noted above that the two basic skills required to coach well are listening and questioning. We look in some detail at these skills in Chapter 7. For the time being, let us consider briefly why these two skills are so important in coaching effectively.

Assume for a moment that you are my manager and that you are using a coaching approach to help me to improve my performance. Why is it important that you listen well?

First, you need to understand my position – how much I already know, where I am struggling, what will interest me, what help I might need, how much time I have, and so on. You can make assumptions about all of these things – or even ignore them – but if you really want me to deliver for you then it is important to check these out. And you can only do that by listening to my views.

Second, if you are going to ask useful questions you need to base these on what I have said. You have to listen to me in order to question me effectively.

There is a third reason why listening well is important. In listening to me, you show me respect, and this will help to build the relationship between us.

If you are listening really effectively, you will not only grasp the meaning of my words but you will also appreciate the emotion behind the words. Emotion is, of course, often conveyed non-verbally. For a simple illustration of non verbal communication, watch a drama or soap on television with the sound off. If the acting is any good, you will be able to follow much of the story without the words.

When listening, you will probably find it very useful to summarise what I have told you. It might be a summary of the most recent part of the conversation or a more general summary of the conversation so far. It can be helpful to signpost a summary with a phrase like *Let me check if I've understood what you're saying.*

A reasonably accurate summary does a number of useful things. It shows me that you have been listening attentively, which in turn can make me feel valued. It enables you to check how well you have understood me, and allows me to correct any misunderstanding on your part. It can sometimes help me as the person being coached to realise that I have been missing something important. When I feel that I am really being listened to, I will probably be more open.

Another attribute of a good listener is the ability to stay quiet during a silence, to feel comfortable with the silence, and not rush in with words to fill the gap. There are many reasons why I may be silent. It is a judgment call by you – perhaps informed by your intuition – as to how long to let a silence go on if I don't break it. It also requires some sensitivity in choosing what to say or do in breaking a silence.

Questioning

When you ask me a really good question, it makes me think. I may think more deeply about something I've just said, or I may look at things from a different perspective, or I may be forced to explore some contradictions in my position, or I may be challenged on how committed I really am – and so on. A good coaching question will either raise my awareness or prompt me to look at my responsibility.

Questioning and listening go hand in hand. If you are coaching me well, your questions will emerge from what I tell you.

Generally speaking, open questions are more useful than closed ones. The open question *What do you like about my proposal?* will prompt a fuller response than the closed question *Do you like my proposal?*

Open questions usually begin with Kipling's trusted friends:

> I keep six honest serving-men
> (They taught me all I knew);
> Their names are *What* and *Why* and *When*
> And *How* and *Where* and *Who*.

Closed questions, on the other hand, begin with a verb. *Is the report at the printers?* or *Can you finish this by Friday?*

Table 2.1 shows a set of alternative questions. Imagine how someone might answer them.

Table 2.1 Closed and open questions

Closed	Open
Was it the signal which caused the accident?	What caused the accident?
Have you finished?	How close are you to finishing?
Do you like this?	What aspects do you like?
Are you supportive?	How supportive are you?
Can you finish the report by Friday?	When can you finish the report?

The open questions will prompt fuller replies whereas all of the closed questions can be answered *yes* or *no*. Occasionally, however, a closed question is highly appropriate – for example, in pinning down a decision: *So, will you speak to him today?*

The word I like to use to describe the right question is *crisp*. A crisp question – simply expressed – helps to focus the speaker on the most useful issue for them at that moment in time. Note that this is more art than science. I could never prove that another question or another phrasing of a question would not have been better still. I just know – or occasionally the speaker will tell me – that I have asked a really useful question.

It can be interesting to observe the questions that television or radio interviewers ask. A good interviewer will ask questions that build on what the speaker has just said. The interviewer has a structure in mind, areas to be covered in the conversation, but is willing to explore as well. A less effective interviewer will have questions written in advance on a clipboard, and will move on in juddering fashion to the next question on the list whatever the speaker says.

The GROW framework

In *Coaching for Performance* John Whitmore sets out a very practical framework for structuring a coaching conversation called the GROW model. This can be summarised as:

Goal	What are you trying to achieve?
Reality	What is currently going on?
Options	What could you do?
Will	What will you do?

It is important to emphasise that the GROW model is not coaching – it is merely a way of structuring a conversation. It can also be used effectively to help a group of people to explore an issue, particularly when they have a shared accountability for addressing this issue. (A heterogeneous group will find it difficult to agree what collectively they will do.) In Chapter 5 we look at how you can use a coaching approach with your team. You can also use the GROW framework on your own to work systematically through an issue and create an action plan.

As you become more skilled in using the GROW structure, you will find that you begin to use it flexibly. With some issues you may spend a lot of time clarifying the goal, and indeed once a problem is stated clearly the solution sometimes becomes obvious. With other issues the goal may be clear but the current reality complex and worthy of considerable exploration. Or you may find that an exploration of reality leads to a restatement of the desired goal. And so on.

There is an excellent exercise which works well on the opening morning of a programme to help managers learn a coaching approach. The exercise – which I call *silent coaching* because the participants are silent – illustrates the GROW model and demonstrates the power of effective questioning.

Each participant identifies a real issue that they would like to spend 20 minutes thinking about. I then ask around 20 questions – around five for each of the four steps of the GROW model – such as those shown in Panel 2.1. Participants simply jot down their individual answers without saying anything. Some questions may not be relevant for some people.

The silent coaching exercise is usually a vivid and thought-provoking demonstration. Generally most of the group make real progress in resolving their issue, simply

Panel 2.1: Typical questions for a silent coaching session

Goal

■ What are you trying to achieve?

■ Imagine that you have successfully addressed your issue.

■ What does success look like?

■ What does success feel like?

■ What do you really, really want?

■ What else would make you delighted with the outcome?

Reality

■ What is going on that makes this an issue for you?

■ Who is involved?

■ What are the key features of the situation?

■ What else is relevant?

■ What – if anything – have you already done to address the situation?

■ And what has been the effect of what you have done so far?

Options

■ What options do you have?

■ What else might you do?

■ If you had a really wise friend, what would they do in your shoes?

■ If you had absolutely no constraints – of time or money or power or health – what would you do?

■ In what other ways could you approach this?

Will

- You have just generated a set of options. Looking back at these options, rate them quickly on a scale of 1 to 10 on how practical they seem.

- Looking over your list of options, which options will you actually pursue?

- For each chosen option, what specifically will you do?

- What deadlines will you set for yourself?

- What help or support do you need?

- Who will suffer if you don't address this issue?

- What is the first step that you will take?

Note how many of the questions begin with *What?* I also find that the very simple question *What else?* – or in conversation the phrase *Tell me more* – often stimulates new thinking or ideas.

---

by thinking in response to 20 open questions chosen to structure their thinking. I find that managers have a real eye-opening experience when they realise the power of asking questions. *How could his questions help me to make such progress with my issue when he didn't even know what my issue was? He certainly didn't – couldn't – tell me what to do.* This is useful as an antidote to *tell.* Managers see that they can be effective without being an expert and without giving advice.

While the silent coaching exercise demonstrates the power of open questions and of the GROW model, it completely misses the benefit of asking the questions that emerge from listening to what the speaker is saying or perhaps communicating non-verbally. Asking the right question at the right time is even more powerful.

The manager coach

If you are a manager who wants to use a coaching approach, you have in many ways a tougher job than someone from outside the organisation working as an executive coach. You have a direct interest in the results delivered by your staff. Your performance may be measured in part by their performance, and you may have strong views on how things should be done. It can be a real challenge to let go of control and use a coaching style to empower your people. On the other hand, while the executive coach is keen for the client to succeed, they do not have the same responsibility for performance as a manager.

It will help both you as the manager and your staff if you are clear about the *givens* in a situation. As a simple illustration, if a report must be ready by Friday, state this clearly and then work in a coaching style with your staff on how this can be done. An inexperienced manager coach can fall into the trap of trying to ask questions to get the staff to the answer they want – in this example, that the report will be done by Friday. This will come across as manipulative and dishonest.

To underline the point, as a manager you need to be clear when you are telling (*I must have the report by Friday*) and when you are coaching (*What might you do in order to finish this by Friday?*).

Another area where a manager has a tougher challenge than an external coach is around confidentiality. Organisations are political institutions in which people earn a living. Even if someone has a sound working relationship with a manager, they will probably and quite wisely put limits on how open and honest they will be. An honest admission of weakness might count against someone next time there is a promotion opportunity. Individuals will usually be more open and honest with a confidant who is outside the organisation.

If you are a line manager using a coaching style you need to balance both halves of the manager coach role. If you can adopt both a *telling* approach and a *listening and questioning approach* – and if you can recognise which situations call for which – then you have more flexibility and will be more effective than a manager who is locked into *tell* only. David Hemery, gold medallist in the 400 metres hurdles at the 1968 Olympics and someone who has helped many managers develop their coaching skills, has created the notion of a *coaching dance*. To be a really effective manager you must be able to move gracefully between telling, on the one hand, and listening and questioning. Moreover, you will do this in a way that leaves people feeling valued, clear about what they are doing and committed to performing excellently.

Hemery's coaching dance is described in Table 2.2. It shows a contrast between a *manager-centred* approach where the manager is *pushing* the performer for results and a *performer-centred* approach where the manager is seeking to *pull* results from the performer.

In a manager-centred approach the manager sets goals and targets. In a performer-centred approach goals and targets are discussed and agreed, and the performer might also set themselves some personal challenges.

In a manager-centred approach the manager uses a variety of carrots and sticks to motivate the performer. In a performer-centred approach the manager will find out from the performer what will motivate or interest them. If appropriate, they will try to build this into the task to be done.

| Table 2.2 | | David Hemery's coaching dance |

Manager-centred (Pushing) (Telling)		Performer-centred (Pulling) (Asking)
Set by the manager	GOALS AND TARGETS	Discuss and agree with performer
Reward and punish Encourage	MOTIVATION	Ask what interests performer Performer challenges self

Pass judgments
Praise and criticise
Give feedback to
    performer
	FEEDBACK	Draw out performer's experience
		Help performer to generate
		    feedback

Tell what went well and
    what didn't
Show how it could have
    been done
	LEARNING	From self awareness
		By reflection and discovery

We look more closely at feedback in the next chapter. For now let us note that the manager-centred manager will give feedback, which is based on their judgment and which may contain a mix of criticism and praise based on this judgment. The performer-centred manager will seek to generate feedback in conversation with the performer, asking first how the performer viewed their performance before adding their own perspective – if this is necessary. People often know when they've made a mistake without having to be told.

Finally, as far as learning goes, the manager-centred manager will be in tell mode, stating how they think the task could have been done better. The performer-centred manager will be helping the performer to clarify and articulate what they think they have learnt.

To underline the point, knowing when to and how to tell someone what to do is a valuable part of a coach's toolkit. For some managers, however, *telling* is the toolkit!

Having experienced the power of a coaching approach during a training programme, managers then have to do two things when they return to work. First, they have to practise and improve their coaching skills because otherwise the learning fades rapidly. (Someone once said that the half-life of training – if it's not used straight away – is around three days.) Second, they need to synthesise their new coaching skills with their previous practice. In other words, they need to do the coaching dance.

Coaching and development reviews

I find that some managers who have attended a coaching workshop find it difficult to deploy a coaching approach in the hurly burly of their everyday job. However, they do find it possible to use their coaching skills in situations such as a performance or development review which by their very nature are set up to be a one-to-one conversation.

The development review form in Figure 2.4 is drafted to invite such a coaching approach. It is simply a series of open questions to raise awareness and encourage responsibility in the individual. Note that the questions put the individual rather than the manager at the centre of the conversation. Note too that the question which asks about work experience deliberately comes before the question about other development actions in order to encourage development solutions which are based on offering real experiences. A new role, a secondment, taking part in a new project, or a fresh and interesting piece of work will create valuable development opportunities, particularly if you also help the individual to reflect upon and learn from the experience.

Figure 2.4 A development review form

YOUR DEVELOPMENT REVIEW

A development review is a conversation between you and your manager to help build your capability. Having a meaningful conversation is more important than completing the paperwork, but you will find the questions below useful to structure the conversation and to provide a record for future reference.

- What are your strengths, both job-related and behavioural?
- What are your weaknesses, both job-related and behavioural?
- What are your aspirations – in the short, medium and long term? What are you prepared to do to achieve these?
- What new experiences or challenges would you like over the next twelve months? What support do you need from your manager?
- In what areas do you want to develop your capability over the next twelve months? In each area, what will you do – and by when – to develop yourself?

3

Giving, generating and gathering feedback

Feedback is the breakfast of champions. (Ken Blanchard)

Introduction

In this chapter I consider the use of feedback to help someone raise their performance and develop their capability. In my view, one of your key tasks as a manager is to encourage people to reflect on and learn from their experiences. Feedback is a catalyst to prompt someone to do this. Relevant feedback can result in changes in performance, behaviour and even attitude. Feedback releases potential.

We begin by looking at *giving and receiving* feedback, which is the customary way of thinking about feedback. We then consider the notion of *generating* feedback, where your task is to help the other person to generate their own feedback on their performance. This approach to feedback fits comfortably with a coaching style of management. We then move on to look at *gathering* feedback where an individual takes responsibility for collecting feedback for themselves.

Giving feedback

The thesaurus on my laptop offers the following synonyms for feedback: criticism, advice, pointer, reaction, comment, response, opinion, view. These words reflect what most people consider as feedback. Feedback is typically about telling someone what you think. It is something that you give and which they receive. This view of feedback fits with a conventional, controlling approach to management.

Giving feedback can be valuable, particularly if it is accurate, specific, timely and offered non-judgmentally. There will be times when it is particularly important to give feedback – for example, when someone is underperforming and is unwilling to face up to or take responsibility for their behaviour.

Many managers find it very difficult to give feedback to others. There are a number of reasons why this might be so. It may be because the manager – and perhaps also the person receiving the feedback – feels uncomfortable about engaging in this kind of conversation, particularly if the feedback is seen as negative. It may be that the manager doesn't have a clear idea of what would constitute effective behaviour and so is unable to offer constructive feedback. Or perceived lack of time may be used as an excuse. As with many aspects of development, however, time invested in the short term repays itself handsomely in the longer term as people grow and take on more responsibility.

Jenny Summerfield contrasts *low-value feedback,* which is empty criticism or praise, and *high-value feedback,* which results in a motivated person who wants to improve their performance. As an illustration, compare these three pieces of feedback:

- Your visual aids are no good.
- Your visual aids are really good.

- Your visual aids are too full of information, which makes the print difficult for people to read.

She suggests a three-part process as the basis for giving high-value feedback:

- Present the facts about the behaviour;
- Explore the effect of the behaviour;
- Present what the person should do differently or do more of.

Note that at any of these three stages you might first invite the other person to state their views before you offer your comments. We shall return to this when we look at generating feedback.

When giving feedback it is worth internally checking your intent before you start to speak. If your intent is actually to vent your feelings of frustration or disappointment, then be clear that this is what you are doing. If your intent is genuinely to help the other person to be more effective next time, then consider carefully what you are going to say. Giving feedback that the other person doesn't hear or accept may release some of your emotions but is unlikely to make any difference to their performance.

Susan Scott talks about the importance of delivering your message *without the load*. Say what you really want to say but avoid dumping a load of your negative feelings or prejudices alongside your message. To deliver your message without the load, you will need to attend both to what you say and how you say it.

Note that this doesn't mean that you don't talk about how you feel in response to the other person's actions. Naming your feelings – for example, *I am very angry about what you did* – will be more helpful than indulging in those emotions during the feedback session.

Jenny Summerfield emphasises the importance of preparing people to receive feedback. She recommends that you consider how best to set things up so that people really hear the feedback and are open to change. She highlights four points in preparing for feedback:

- The culture of the organisation – or the department – needs to be right. Weaknesses have to be seen as development needs, not as failures or something to be punished for. If this condition is present, it removes a lot of the fear associated with feedback.

- The person receiving the feedback should be aware of their own inner dialogue. What are the conversations that typically go on inside their head when they hear something negative – or even positive – about themselves? Naming and putting to one side the inner dialogue enables the message within the feedback to be heard more clearly and without prejudice.

- The individual usually knows – in their heart of hearts – what is going wrong. Feedback can often be a relief, and provides the platform for change.

- Remember that feedback that confirms strengths is worth giving too – not as a way of softening negative feedback, but rather because it is often important to tell people that they are doing well.

Generating feedback

We saw in the previous chapter that when coaching someone, you are trying to do two things – to raise their awareness and to encourage them to take responsibility. A danger in giving feedback is that – even when the other person apparently accepts what you are saying – they do not really grasp the point. Moreover, even if they fully understand the feedback they may not be committed to doing anything as a result.

An alternative to *giving* feedback is *generating* feedback. Using your listening and questioning skills, your role is to encourage the other person to generate their own feedback on how they have performed. When they generate their own feedback, they will be more aware of what they did and be more likely to take responsibility for performing differently next time.

In *Coaching for Performance,* John Whitmore writes that, 'Generating high-quality relevant feedback, as far as possible from within rather than from experts, is essential for continuous improvement, at work, in sport and in all aspects of life' (Whitmore, 2002).

He then illustrates five levels of feedback used by a manager commenting on a report that someone has written. These are detailed in Table 3.1

In his view, only the last form of feedback is likely to improve performance and promote learning. The open questions promote both awareness and responsibility on the part of the performer, which in turn produces performance and learning.

Here are some illustrative questions to help someone to generate feedback for themselves on a piece of work. These are generally open questions that encourage exploration. There is no need to ask all of the questions, and they can be modified to suit the actual situation. Note that your questions will be even more effective when they flow from what the individual has just said.

- What are you pleased about in this piece of work? Less pleased about?

- On a scale of 1 to 10, how satisfied are you? What would have made it a 10?

- What would you do differently next time?

- What have you learnt from doing this project?

- What patterns do you notice about how you did this task and how you have tackled other tasks?

Your ability to engage in the kind of conversation that helps someone to generate feedback for themselves will depend on the quality of the relationship between the two of you. There needs to be a degree of openness and trust in the

Table 3.1   John Whitmore's five levels of feedback

Feedback	Effect
You are useless	Personalised criticism that damages confidence and contains nothing helpful
This report is useless	Judgmental comment that damages confidence and contains no useable information
The content is clear but the layout is messy	Some information but no ownership by the performer
How do you feel about the report?	Encourages ownership but likely to prompt a vague response or a value judgment (such as *fine, lousy*)
What is the essential purpose of the report? To what extent does this draft achieve that? What other points need to be emphasised? etc	The performer gives a detailed non-judgmental description

relationship. We will be looking in later chapters at the nature of the relationships you establish with your people and at the kind of conversations you create.

If after reviewing a piece of work the performer is still missing something important, you may wish to point this out. This is best done after first questioning. You may well find that there is no need for you to add anything because the performer identifies all of the key points themselves.

While it is valuable to help someone to generate their own feedback, there will nevertheless be times when it is essential that you tell someone what you think about their performance or behaviour. When someone is underperforming – or when someone's behaviour or style of interacting with others is causing offence – it is part of your role as a manager to address this explicitly with the individual. You may well find that you need to state clearly, with supporting evidence, what the person is doing wrong.

Feedforward

John Whitmore also talks about *feedforward* – that is, helping someone prepare for and plan a piece of work. Here are some examples of feedforward questions:

- What is the purpose of this task?
- What will success look like?
- What information do you need?
- What are you concerned about?
- Who can help?
- What are the key steps along the way?
- How shall we review this?

- In which areas are you looking for feedback on your performance?

The final question can be a very useful one to ask at the start of a piece of work. It can help the individual to focus on what they want to do more effectively, and it tells you what to watch out for in order to structure a follow-up feedback session. For example, the performer may want feedback on how clearly they communicate, and you can explicitly ask them about this in a review.

Gathering feedback

We have just looked at going beyond *giving* feedback to *generating* feedback. Further still is the idea of *gathering* feedback, where the individual actively sets out to collect information that will enhance their development or performance.

For example, you might want proactively to seek feedback on your management style. Begin by identifying those around you whose views you respect, who are likely to have valuable insights into your behaviour, and who will be willing to let you know how they see your management style. Seek out these people and ask for their feedback. It may be easier to ask people to write down their views in answer to some structured questions. You might follow this up by meeting some of them to clarify their views and to check out important aspects of the feedback.

The exercise in Panel 3.1 illustrates how you might gather feedback to help you to clarify your role and to better meet the expectations of your key stakeholders. Note that the final, analysis stage of the exercise is a form of self-coaching.

Panel 3.1: Role analysis exercise

1. Preparation

Choose half a dozen people whom you would like to complete the questionnaire below. You will gain most benefit by choosing people who:

- have significant interactions with you at work
- view you from different perspectives (e.g. boss, report, customer)
- will give you their honest views

Give the questionnaire to each of your chosen respondents, asking them for their help. It is useful to suggest a deadline not too far in the future – say, in a week's time. Ask them to return the questionnaire to you. You may wish to meet some of your respondents to explore their views in more detail.

Complete the separate self questionnaire on how you see your own role. It is important that you do this before you have seen any other replies.

2. Questionnaire

Your colleague would like your views to help them to clarify their role and to meet effectively the needs of their key stakeholders. You will be of most help if you answer honestly and fully.

- In a sentence, what do you consider to be the main purpose of this person's role?
- From your position, what are your main expectations of this person in terms of what you expect them to deliver?

- From your own perspective, what are the key behaviours you expect this person to demonstrate at work?

3. Self questionnaire

- In a sentence, summarise the main purpose of your role.

- List what you see as the key aspects of your role. Roughly what percentage of your working time do you think you should be devoting to each aspect?

- By reflecting on some reasonably typical weeks – or, better still, by completing a log as you go through a typical week – estimate what percentage of your working time you actually spend on these and on any other aspects that take a significant proportion of your working time.

4. Analysis

- What are the main differences between how you see the purpose of your role and how others see it?

- What are the main differences between how you spend your working time and the key aspects of your role?

- What are the main differences between how you spend your working time and what others expect you to deliver?

- What surprises you about the behaviours that others expect you to demonstrate at work?

- What do you want to do differently?

- What conversations will you have following this exercise?

360-degree feedback

Many organisations today use 360-degree feedback to help individuals to review how other people see their performance or behaviour or style. It is called 360-degree feedback because the feedback is given by people from all around the individual – boss, peers, subordinates, and possibly customers or suppliers. The person also assesses themselves so that they can compare their views with the perceptions of those around them. The role analysis exercise is in effect a simple 360-degree feedback process built around a few open questions.

360-degree feedback is generally gathered via a questionnaire. Questionnaires may be tailored to reflect the organisation's competency or values framework, or a more generic off-the-shelf instrument may be used. In the past the questionnaires and reports were usually paper-based but it is now straightforward to make the process electronic, often via the Internet.

Generally the individual chooses who will complete the questionnaire, although it is usual to specify that one respondent must be their line manager. Some people may select those whom they are confident will say good things about them. Much more valuable feedback will come from people who, first of all, know the individual well enough and, second, will be honest with their responses whether positive or negative.

Some organisations use 360-degree feedback as part of their performance management process. If performance reviews are linked to pay or bonuses then the individual may select respondents who view them favourably. Moreover, some respondents may not be as honest as they would be if the feedback were being gathered for developmental purposes. My own view is that 360-degree feedback is best positioned as a development opportunity for which individuals can volunteer, not as an input to performance rating, pay or promotion.

Questionnaires can also ask people for comments on the individual which will be fed back verbatim but anonymously in the report. Comments might, for example, be invited on strengths and weaknesses, or on *should do more of* and *should do less of*. These reported comments are often the most thought-provoking part of the feedback.

It is important to reassure respondents that their ratings and comments will not be attributed to them personally (except for the ratings given by the line manager which are usually separated out in the report). Using an external agency to receive responses and to create the feedback report will convince most people – though not all – that their responses are confidential.

You can in fact dispense with a questionnaire completely and use only textual comments, as in the role analysis exercise. But many people like to see the graphs comparing their own views with others'. Note, however, the risk that a well laid out feedback report with coloured charts gives a spurious impression of accuracy and objectivity. Remember that 360-degree feedback is based on subjective views. It isn't a precise assessment. Like other forms of feedback, it is a catalyst to stimulate reflection, learning and action planning.

Once the questionnaires have been analysed and a feedback report prepared, it is more valuable to have a facilitator take the individual through the report in a face-to-face meeting than to send the report to the individual by post or electronically. The facilitator can help the individual, first, to digest the feedback and, second, to create an action plan to enhance performance or develop capability. Here are some open questions you might use to coach someone seeking to create an action plan following 360-degree feedback:

- What do you see as the main themes in your feedback?
- Given your current role and your aspirations for the future, what development goals do you want to set yourself?
- What steps will you take to achieve each of these goals?
- What support will you need and from whom?
- What deadlines will you set yourself?
- When and how will you review progress?

4

Mentoring

Everyone needs a mentor. (David Clutterbuck)

Introduction

In this chapter I shift the focus from you as a line manager helping your people to learn from their experience, to you as a mentor supporting the development of people who do not directly report to you. I will also consider more generally how to establish mentoring as a key development process in an organisation.

What is mentoring?

Informal relationships where someone with experience helps a younger person exist in many settings. Mentoring has been around since the time of the ancient Greeks – and doubtless before that. According to Greek mythology, when Odysseus set out for Troy he left the education of his son Telemachus to his friend Mentor – from whom we get the word *mentor*.

The terms coaching and mentoring are often confused, and there is no generally agreed definition of which is which. When I use the term *mentor* in this book, I mean a more experienced person outside the normal line management relationship who acts as a combination of sounding board and giver of advice born from their own experience. A mentor may come from either within or outside the organisation. This leads to the following definition:

> Mentoring is a non-judgmental relationship, outside the normal line management relationship, where a more experienced person helps another to enhance his or her performance, learning or development.

The executive coaching firm CPS uses the words 'coaching' and 'mentoring' more or less exactly opposite to how I have defined them. What I call *coaching* they call *mentoring*, and vice versa. Although a little confusing, it doesn't really matter as long as we are clear what we mean.

There are a number of points to highlight in this definition. First and foremost, mentoring – like coaching – is a *relationship*.

Second, I am regarding mentoring as a relationship *outside the line*. A line manager can of course act as a mentor. In *Leading People,* Penny van Eupen and Amin Rajan report that a key factor that helped leaders to learn their art was that:

> they had good mentors at work, whose real worth only became evident long after the encounter. In the earlier part of their careers, mentors tended to be their immediate supervisors. Over time, some leaders acquired external mentors. (van Eupen and Rajan, 1996)

However, there can be tension or conflict between a manager's role as mentor and their role as boss with responsibility for discipline, appraisal and salary increases. Moreover, it is often the case that the issue which needs to be worked through is the relationship between the individual and their manager. Thus, when I speak of a mentor in this book, I mean the use of a third party outside the line.

Third, there is the question of whether the role of the mentor includes the sharing of experience and advice, or whether the mentor is non-directive. In my terms I expect the mentor to offer experience and advice, but in the knowledge that they will often be of more help, particularly in the medium and long term, if their preference is to let the mentee work out their own solutions. (The English language lacks a suitable word here and I shall use the unlovely term *mentee* to refer to the person being mentored.)

Where mentoring is particularly useful

Mentoring can be a valuable experience at many points in a career, helping someone to:

- learn by reflecting on their experience
- tackle performance challenges
- improve difficult relationships
- plan their career
- develop confidence and skills

In principle, everyone – as the title of David Clutterbuck's book *Everyone Needs a Mentor* suggests – could benefit from having a mentor. However, there are some particular situations where mentoring can be especially useful.

Mentoring can help people to break through real or perceived glass ceilings. For example, some organisations run a mentoring scheme to help female employees to clarify their career aspirations, to think through the balancing of work and non-work priorities, to question unspoken norms within a male-dominated culture, to build confidence, and to create personal career development plans. Often the mentor will be a more senior female manager, who may act as a role model of what it takes for a woman to succeed in that organisation.

Mentoring is useful with young, talented managers who are seen as having the potential to go far within an organisation. Similar issues are likely to arise here too – themes such as self-belief, managing oneself within a culture, preparing to meet new challenges, clarifying goals, making and implementing action plans, and learning from day-to-day experiences.

A particular example of this is in helping graduate entrants make the transition from college to the world of work. The mentor can help the graduate not only to deal with the transition but to think about future career paths and issues such as how to be assertive in this new environment or how to manage a boss effectively. Graduate retention is a problem in many organisations, and a meaningful mentoring relationship can help talented young people to work through issues that might otherwise contribute to their leaving the organisation.

Mentoring can also be useful for more experienced people in certain situations. For example, it can help someone who has recently joined the organisation from outside, or who has taken on a significantly different role, to find their feet more quickly in their new situation. Alternatively, it may be used to help someone who is technically very capable but struggling to build productive working relationships or to influence effectively. In many senior roles, technical skills are not enough, and it may be the case that the individual can only succeed if they can add behavioural competence to their technical expertise.

The benefits of being a mentor

Although the primary purpose in a mentoring relationship is to help the mentee, you will find that you too gain from the experience of being a mentor. Being a mentor offers a number of benefits. (Note that these might be useful in trying to attract volunteers to become mentors.)

First, there is the real satisfaction in helping another person – probably a younger person – to learn and grow in confidence and self-esteem. In many organisations today with a sharp focus on bottom line results and performance, it is easy to lose sight of the value of simply helping someone.

Second, mentors are playing a part in building the future capability of the organisation by developing some of its talented people.

Third, acting as a mentor gives you a real-time opportunity to practise and enhance your coaching skills. Your ability to listen and question, to support and challenge, to be non-directive and non-judgmental are valuable both as a mentor and as a line manager using a coaching approach with your people.

Fourth, listening with empathy to your mentee – seeing the world through their eyes – affords you a fresh perspective on the world. This might stimulate all sorts of insights – into personal and business issues – for you. In a mentoring relationship, the mentor is a learner too and, in some cases, may gain more from the process than the mentee.

More generally, if mentoring becomes a widely accepted feature within an organisation, this can help to shift its culture to one where self-development, developing others and taking part in meaningful, reflective conversations are genuinely valued. This in turn contributes to an environment where people feel good about their work and their organisation.

What makes a good mentor?

Not everyone is suitable as a mentor, and some very senior people – if they are autocratic or very judgmental or simply fascinated by the sound of their own voice – can be particularly unsuitable.

The following qualities are useful attributes to look for in choosing mentors:

- A mundane but vital consideration is that the potential mentor has the time available to meet regularly – say, for an hour every four to six weeks – with their mentee. If they are mentoring more than one person, this obviously needs to be allowed for too. The most skilful mentor in the organisation is of little use if they do not spend time with the mentee.

- A mentor must be able to build the right kind of relationship with their mentee. They must have good listening skills. They must be able to offer both support and challenge. They must be able to work both non-judgmentally and non-directively, giving the mentee the space to try things out in their own way and, if necessary, learn from their mistakes. The mentor needs to be able to share their own experiences in a way that leaves the mentee free to take what they want to use and leave what they do not. It follows that someone with a command and control, telling style of management will struggle to be an effective mentor.

- A mentor needs to be able to respect confidentiality.

- A mentor needs to be interested both in their own learning and development and in supporting the learning and development of others. If a senior manager has a reputation for not being particularly good at developing their own staff, why would they be any better at developing someone else's?

- It is also useful if the mentor has a positive but realistic view of the world.

It is also worth thinking about the selection of mentees, particularly if there are more people looking to be mentored than can be accommodated by the number of available mentors. A basic consideration is how likely the individual is to benefit from having a mentor. Someone who is unwilling to talk about themselves, or who has inflexible views, or who isn't interested in developing themselves is much less likely to benefit than someone who is open, flexible and keen to learn. It may be too that the organisation wishes to focus on the needs of a particular group, such as graduate entrants, women or ethnic minorities.

The mentoring relationship

Since mentoring is about the development of the mentee, it is important that you as the mentor allow the mentee to take as much responsibility as possible for managing the relationship. Remember that the mentee sets the agenda. Although this may be stated clearly at an initial briefing, nevertheless the mentee may still be looking for direction from you. Equally, you as the mentor may feel you ought to be giving a steer.

I would encourage you, therefore, in the early stages of the relationship to resist the temptation to jump in and solve things. This will create a dependency and implicitly set the ground rules for the relationship. Instead, keep firmly in mind that you are establishing a relationship where the mentee takes the lead.

Typically, a mentoring relationship will progress through a number of stages. The following outline is based on the work of David Clutterbuck:

- *Establishing rapport:* exchanging expectations and agreeing how to work together.

- *Setting direction:* determining and prioritising the mentee's initial needs and goals.

- *Making progress:* addressing the mentee's issues, reviewing progress, and identifying new ways of working.

- *Moving on:* reviewing what has been learnt that can be used in the future, and allowing the relationship to end or evolve.

You may find that at the end of a formal mentoring arrangement you and your mentee agree to carry on meeting on a less formal basis. Some mentoring relationships continue – perhaps off and on – over many years.

Guidelines for an internal mentoring scheme

This section sets out some guidelines to consider when setting up a mentoring scheme within an organisation. I am indebted to Deana Hirst (an associate of David Clutterbuck) and my ex-colleague Will Large for the work that shaped these guidelines.

- Participation – both of mentees and mentors – must be voluntary. I strongly urge you not to compromise on this.

As with all learning opportunities, if a mentee doesn't want to take part then the chances of success are hugely reduced. Similarly, if a mentor doesn't really want to do this, then they are unlikely to find the time let alone the commitment to make the relationship really work. Moreover, if word spreads that some mentoring relationships aren't working, then mentoring begins to get a bad name within the organisation.

- Mentees and mentors need a clear understanding of the purpose of the scheme, their respective roles and responsibilities, and any ground rules that are given. A clear definition of mentoring – such as the one offered earlier – helps here. It is useful to hold an initial briefing session for mentors and mentees.

- Offer mentors training in coaching skills to help them engage in high-quality conversations with their mentees.

- Allow each mentee some say in choosing their mentor. You will be unable to let each mentee state who will mentor them – for example, what if everyone chooses the same person? However, the mentee should be able to indicate some preference – perhaps, first, second and third choice – from the pool of available mentors, and have the right to turn down a proposed mentor.

- There are a number of practical issues in matching. A simple but important one is geography. Unless the scheme is some kind of distance mentoring via phone and e-mail, the mentor and mentee will meet regularly. There is great merit in making this as convenient as possible. Another potential issue in matching is gender – for example, a woman may prefer to be mentored by another woman. There may be a desire in some circumstances to match people from similar disciplines or ethnic origin. And so on.

- Permit either party to break off the relationship without blame or fault or detailed explanation – and to continue in a fresh mentoring relationship if appropriate.

- Set up mentoring relationships for a fixed duration – say, nine or twelve months – with an end point set at the outset. It may be that mentor and mentee continue to meet informally beyond the duration of the formal scheme.

- A manager acting as an internal mentor can usually only take on one or two mentees at a time.

- The line managers of those being mentored need to understand the purpose of the scheme and appreciate how their role fits with the mentor's. A line manager still has a vital part to play in supporting the development of someone who has an off-line mentor.

- Build in a review of the process at the mid-point to enable mentors and mentees to come together as a group, share experiences and refocus their practice. A closing review can also help to capture and share learning.

- There needs to be a programme manager in overall charge of the mentoring scheme. Their responsibilities might include:

  - Assessing the suitability of potential mentors;
  - Arranging briefings and training for mentors and mentees;
  - Matching mentors and mentees;
  - Acting as a sounding board for mentors or mentees if they want to review how mentoring is working out for them;
  - Making the necessary arrangements when either party wishes to break off the relationship;

- Monitoring the effectiveness of the mentoring;
- Introducing ways of continually improving the scheme.

Is the mentor a sponsor?

A mentor can be of enormous benefit to a mentee simply by helping them to address their current challenges, learn from their experiences and consider their future direction. In the security of an effective mentoring relationship, a mentee can grow in confidence, self-belief and possibly ambition.

It is not necessary that the mentor act as a sponsor within the organisation to promote their mentee. In some mentoring schemes, however, this is part of the expectation. If so, it is important that there is clarity on all sides about the role.

If the mentor is expected to act as a sponsor – for example, by acting as an advocate for their mentee in succession discussions – then this is another factor to be considered by the mentee when indicating whom they would like as a mentor. Indeed, the politically astute mentee may opt for seniority and influence within the company as the key criteria that they seek in a mentor, rather than someone who will support their learning. The ideal mentor sponsor will, of course, be able both to support learning and be an effective advocate.

A mentor acting as a sponsor may at times share with management colleagues their views of the mentee and possibly some of the issues concerning the mentee. It may be, therefore, that not everything discussed between the mentee and mentor can be treated as confidential. If this is the case, then the mentee needs to consider how open to be with the mentor, which will inevitably limit the scope and effectiveness of the mentoring relationship. I have spoken to one mentee who understood that his mentor would talk about him during talent reviews. Hence he only told the mentor things he was willing to have repeated. It is doubtful if there was much new learning in this relationship.

As this example illustrates, there is inevitably tension in a scheme where senior people mentor individuals and also discuss these individuals in talent management or selection meetings.

Alternatives to mentoring

In this section I describe briefly three other ways of offering people an opportunity to work through issues facing them and to learn from their day-to-day experience – executive coaching, peer mentoring and action learning.

Executive coaching

Someone in a senior position near the top of an organisation may be unwilling to discuss the personal or business issues they are facing with another party within the organisation. The use of specialised external coaches is currently a popular form of support for the performance or development of key people, including top executives. Such coaching can be more focused and timely than other types of development support.

This is often referred to as executive coaching. Note, in passing, the comment of one coach about the term: 'I think it's called executive coaching because it's posher and you can get more money for it. I also coach unemployed people'.

The use of an external person brings several advantages:

- The executive is far more likely to trust that the relationship is confidential, and so will be more likely to open up about what is really going on for them or their organisation.

- Consequently the coaching can concentrate on the areas that will make the greatest difference to the executive's performance.

- As a specialist, the external coach is likely to bring a far higher level of skill and experience to the coaching role than an internal line manager or mentor can.

- The coach is likely to have support in the form of a supervisor – that is, someone with whom they can review their coaching.

- The coach may have more ready access to specialist assistance in technical areas – for example, corporate finance or personal impact – if this is needed to supplement the coaching conversations.

The main downside in using an external coach is that it is expensive. A year's coaching support to an executive might cost upwards of £15,000. This cost needs to be balanced against the potential benefits from having an executive who is more confident, aware and effective.

Peer mentoring

In peer mentoring two people meet regularly to mentor each other, sharing the time between them. Each helps the other to work through their agenda. This can be a simple and inexpensive way to help people to reflect on their experiences and to tackle the challenges facing them. It may be the most practical way to proceed if you don't have enough suitable people to act as mentors.

One way of using peer mentoring is within a management development programme to help to transfer the learning back to the workplace. Participants can be encouraged to pair up, share their action plans with one another, and then meet, phone or e-mail to support each other in carrying out their plans.

Action learning

In *Action Learning for Managers* Mike Pedler offers the following definition:

> Action Learning is a method for individual and organisational development. Working in small groups, people tackle important organisational issues or problems and learn from their attempts to change things. (Pedler, 1996)

In action learning individuals are trying to solve real problems. Whether or not they solve the problem in a sense does not really matter – the key aim is to learn from attempting to solve the problem.

Action learning typically involves a group of half a dozen or so members, generally but not always with a facilitator. An action learning set typically meets every four to six weeks for between a couple of hours and a day. The group divides the available time between each of the members so that everyone gets an opportunity to focus on their issue.

Some groups decide to split the time equally among all of the members, though others work more flexibly. This is usually one of the ground rules that a set establishes early on. Another ground rule may cover confidentiality, where usually it is important that what is said in the meeting goes no further without express permission.

When a set member is discussing their issue, the role of the others is somewhat similar to that of a mentor or coach – to listen and ask questions which help to raise awareness and encourage the individual to take responsibility for acting. The other set members offer support and challenge. Their role is not to offer their solutions unless requested.

A member of an action learning set thus has to work in two ways. First, they need to work through issues which really matter to them, where they do not know how to proceed, and which they genuinely want to tackle. Second, they need to help each of their set colleagues to address their issues.

Action learning sets are another way of encouraging people on a management development programme to put their learning into practice back at work and to continue their development journey.

Developing teams and organisations

Of a good leader, who talks little, when his work is done, his aims fulfilled, they will all say, *We did this ourselves*. (Lao Tse)

Introduction

In this chapter I look at how you can use a coaching style of leadership to help your team to perform effectively and to develop their capability. I also consider what it means to be a team rather than merely a group of individuals who work together, and outline a model of how teams develop. Finally, I offer a definition of a learning organisation and set out a practical way of helping your team become one by systematically learning from its experience.

Coaching a team

We saw in Chapter 2 how as a manager you can use a coaching approach to help one of your people to perform and develop. In a similar way you can use a coaching approach with the group of people that you lead. The key ideas are just the same when coaching a team or coaching an individual. Your two fundamental tasks are to raise awareness in the team and to encourage responsibility. Similarly, the two basic skills you need are listening and questioning.

Because you are dealing with a number of people, coaching a team is more complicated than coaching an individual. There may be complex group dynamics going on within the team that affect how it operates and which might be difficult to fully understand. In *Effective Coaching* Myles Downey talks about

> the obvious distinction between individual and team coaching: there are more people involved. At the surface level this means that more time is spent in the process of coaching. An individual can get to a level of clarity and make a decision relatively quickly. In a team that process takes much more time as each person needs to be heard, disagreement handled, consensus and commitment built. Now look beyond the surface, look to the interrelationships in the team, the dynamics and evolution of the team, and a whole new ball game emerges. (Downey, 2003)

You can very effectively use the GROW model with your team to structure discussions during team meetings:

- Goal: *What do we want to achieve?* When they approach a new task, different members of the team may have different views on what the team's goal should be, and you need a way of making a decision on this. There will be times when you as the leader will decide, and on other occasions you may be looking for some form of consensus to emerge.

- *Reality: What is the current situation?* Different people may regard different aspects of the current reality as important. As we shall explore in Chapter 7, it is helpful if people can appreciate the validity and value of multiple perspectives rather than arguing for one right way of seeing the world.

- *Options: What could we do?* It may in fact be easier to generate options as a group precisely because people see things differently and, moreover, they can build on one another's ideas.

- *Will: What will we do?* It is sometimes very difficult for a group to make a collective decision about what they are going to do. You can of course decide for the group, but be clear that this is what you are doing. It may be that you get agreement when you really want commitment. As when coaching individuals, you have more choices when you can flexibly and appropriately use both a *telling* approach – where you make the decision – and a *listening and questioning* approach – where you let the group decide.

Just as feedback is valuable for an individual, it is also useful for a team. As the leader there will be times when you decide to *give* feedback to your team. However, you can also use appropriate questions to help your team to *generate* feedback on their performance or encourage them to *gather* feedback from, for example, customers. The team development exercise set out later in the chapter encourages everyone to say what qualities will make the team successful and then to rate the team against these. An exercise like this is one way of helping your team to generate feedback for itself.

As the manager of a team, you will sometimes be working with the group and sometimes with individuals. There may also be natural sub-teams within the overall team that you work with. Your success as a leader in getting the best out of your people will reflect how well you build constructive working relationships with each of them. We shall be looking at creating effective relationships in the next chapter.

In the same way that you offer challenging experiences to help individuals develop, you also need to spot opportunities that will provide your team with fresh challenges and help them to learn from their experience. At the end of this chapter we consider how your team might systematically tackle new pieces of work and then review in order to learn and improve.

Before moving on, let's consider what it means to be a team rather than merely a group of individuals.

What is a team?

Some time ago I acted as facilitator to the management team of a support services department. It consisted of the heads of various support departments within the business, such as finance, human resources (HR), communications and legal, together with their boss, the director of support services. For a long time this group struggled to get their heads round what it meant for them to be a team. I recall one session where they tried unsuccessfully to craft a meaningful mission statement for the department.

In *The Wisdom of Teams,* Jon Katzenbach and Douglas Smith offer a definition of a team that explains just why that support services management team had struggled:

> A team is a small number of people with complementary skills committed to a common purpose, performance goals and ways of working together for which they

hold themselves mutually accountable. (Katzenbach and Smith, 1994)

The support services management group – although they played important roles in helping the business to succeed and although they had a need to communicate certain information to one other – were not mutually accountable for achieving shared goals. The finance manager had his responsibilities, the head of legal had different responsibilities. There was no call for them to be a team. They were simply a group of individuals who had to work with a degree of alignment in the interests of the business and who reported to the same director. They could have saved themselves enormous time, energy and angst had they realised that they did not need to be a team.

A similar point is made in an article called 'Second Thoughts on Team Building' by Bill Critchley and David Casey, who realised while running a team-building event with the top management group of an organisation that, 'For most of their time this group of people had absolutely no need to work as a team; indeed the attempt to do so was causing more puzzlement and scepticism than motivation and commitment' (Critchley and Casey, 1984).

They emphasise that the top group does need to function as a team when they are creating strategy for the organisation. The creation of a business strategy is a shared task for which they are mutually accountable, and so – as we see from Katzenbach and Smith's definition – they need to be a team when they are setting strategy. For most of the time, however, the finance director will be doing quite different things from the HR director, and so on. They will need to speak to each other, and from time to time subgroups will need to come together, but most of the time they don't need to be a team.

I find this definition extremely liberating, and encourage you to consider which groups that you belong to or lead are genuinely teams and which are not. If you are involved in a group whose members are not mutually accountable for achieving common goals, you and your colleagues can feel okay about not engaging in 'teamy' things. You may not need to know the detail of everyone's plans, for example. Nor do you need to go on away days together in the pursuit of team building. Instead, you can each focus on achieving your departmental goals and concentrate your team-building efforts with the groups that genuinely do need to be a team.

Stages of team development

There are a variety of models of how teams develop. The model that makes most sense to me is one you will find in David Whitaker's book, *The Spirit of Teams,* or in John Whitmore's book, *Coaching for Performance.* Whitaker in particular has vast experience of teams through his days as an international hockey player, as coach of the British men's hockey team which won the Olympic gold medal in Seoul in 1988, and as a coach to executive teams in business.

The three stages in this model that teams go through as they develop are:

- inclusion
- assertion
- cooperation.

In the *inclusion* stage, people are gauging to what extent they are included in the group. They may be feeling insecure, and possibly asking themselves if they want to be in this group. Some people will deal with their anxiety about acceptance or rejection by being quiet or tentative, while others may compensate by being vocal or forceful.

In the *assertion* stage, people who feel included begin to assert themselves in order to stake a claim for their territory within the group and their place in the pecking order. There may be power struggles and lots of competition within the group. This can make the group productive. Many groups do not advance beyond this stage.

In the *cooperation* stage, people who feel established begin to support each other and to trust each other. There is a lot of commitment to the team, patience and understanding of each other, and humour and enthusiasm. There is also a willingness to challenge ideas and debate issues constructively. The team is aligned well towards the achievement of its goals.

Note that it is entirely possible that a team will slip backwards at times to earlier stages of development. I like the way that the three stages are linked to the feelings and behaviours of individual members, which strikes me as a realistic basis for a model of group development. If someone new joins a team – even one that is cooperative – they will still need to go through the inclusion and assertion stages, and this might affect how others behave.

You might like to review whether your own team is at the inclusion or assertion or cooperation stage. Or you might consider where each member of your team stands at the moment. This may suggest issues that you need to address or conversations you ought to have with individuals or the team as a whole. Similarly, you might reflect on where you stand in relation to some of the teams that you yourself are a member of.

A team development exercise

I really like exercises which offer a simple structure and invite people to look at their own experiences against this framework. For example, I might invite someone to draw a line of any description which represents their life to date and mark on it key events. Talking over their lifeline with someone else can be very revealing for the individual.

The exercise in Panel 5.1 offers a framework to engage your team in a conversation to identify and build the qualities that will make it successful. The exercise enables the team, first, to articulate the qualities needed in an effective team and, second, to assess itself against its own template. Within this structure, all of the content comes from the members of the team based on their own experiences. Moreover, the exercise structures the conversation to encourage everyone to contribute. You can of course create your own variations of the different steps.

Panel 5.1: A team development exercise

Step one

Individually, from your first-hand experiences of working in or leading a team, write down the qualities that you believe characterise a high performing team.

The facilitator – or a member of the group who also is a participant in the exercise – goes round the group asking each person in turn to name one quality that is important to them. This continues until all of the qualities are captured on a flipchart.

Step two

As a group, discuss these and identify the half a dozen qualities that will be most useful for this team.

The facilitator lists the agreed key qualities on a flipchart.

Step three

Individually, rate the team's performance on a 1–10 scale against each quality – both current performance and desired future performance. (Not all qualities need ideally be a 10 – you can get too much of a good thing.)

The facilitator captures these ratings on a flipchart.

Step four

As a group, consider the ratings. You may wish to focus particularly on those qualities where:

■ the individual ratings vary most

■ there are big gaps between current and desired performance.

Once the ratings against each quality have been discussed, the facilitator then coaches the team to identify what goals they want to set about how they will work together, and what actions they will commit to in order to achieve these goals. It is helpful to record goals and actions, circulate these after the meeting, and monitor progress.

Step five

Individually, note what you personally will do differently to bring more of these key qualities to the team.

The facilitator might ask each person in turn to state one thing that they are committed to doing differently.

A learning organisation

Peter Senge's book *The Fifth Discipline,* which has the subtitle *The Art & Practice of The Learning Organisation,* was published in 1990. For a time it became fashionable in companies to talk about becoming a learning organisation. The fashion seems to have passed, leaving behind a view that this was merely another fad. I think this is unfortunate. I'd like now to consider the notion of a learning organisation from the perspective that learning requires experience together with reflection on that experience.

When I first began thinking about a learning organisation, I found it difficult to get my head round the notion that an organisation could learn. After all, learning takes place in individual heads and hearts and bodies. Individuals learn. What does it mean to say that a collection of people – a team or an organisation – learns?

When we speak of a learning organisation we are using a metaphor which contains within it the comparison of an organisation with an individual. A metaphor is a way of understanding one thing through a comparison with another. Such a comparison is always partial, and what matters in not the truth of the metaphor but the richness of the insights it offers. (We look at metaphors in more detail in the next chapter.)

Thinking of the concept of a learning organisation as simply a metaphor helps to clarify the fuzziness surrounding the term. We can take David Kolb's definition of learning from experience – which is the basis of this book – and create a definition of a learning organisation.

Organisations exist to achieve goals and, as Peter Honey says, 'The great end of learning is not knowledge but action'. So, combining this notion with the Kolb definition suggests the following:

A learning organisation is one which transforms its experience to create knowledge, and uses this knowledge to achieve or revise its goals.

As an illustration of organisation learning from experience, consider a classic business school case study of how a small team of Japanese executives established Honda in the US motorcycle market. Their market research suggested that large-engined bikes would sell best in the USA. While they were unsuccessfully attempting to sell these bikes, they themselves travelled round California on small 50cc bikes. These attracted much attention, and the Honda executives were smart enough, first, to appreciate the significance of this and, second, to alter their strategy to one of selling small bikes. This story can be viewed in different ways, but one perspective is to say that the Honda team learnt from its early experiences in the USA how to successfully penetrate the US motorcycle market.

Organisational memory: storing and retrieving knowledge

The usefulness of a metaphor depends upon the insights it offers. You can play with the metaphor of a learning organisation in various ways. For example, learning leads to knowledge and this knowledge has to be stored and retrieved. When an individual learns, they store the new knowledge in their brain or body. They remember what they have learnt, and retrieve this from memory when required. Both storage and retrieval are done by the individual.

We might ask, therefore, how does a learning organisation store and retrieve knowledge? In other words, how does an organisation develop a memory?

One way is inside individual heads. The experienced accountant knows, for example, how to assess an investment proposal, the HR manager knows about wage bargaining, and so on. A problem arises when individuals leave the organisation because, if the knowledge is only their heads, then it's lost to the organisation – a case of memory loss.

Storing information inside individual heads, though commonplace, does not fully answer the question, 'how does an organisation store and retrieve knowledge?'. Here are a number of other answers.

One way is to embody learning – say, from research into new technology or from a better understanding of customer needs – in innovative products. Learning becomes encapsulated in improved products or services.

A second way that organisations store knowledge is through systems and procedures. A schedule of delivery routes, a disciplinary procedure, a budget setting and reporting process, and the like, are all ways of embodying past learning in routines. There is no problem of retrieval in this case, although outdated systems may no longer serve a revised set of objectives.

A third way of storing learning is through the culture of the organisation – that is, the way we do things round here. This information is generally less tangible than that involved in routines. Acceptable behaviour, the things we talk about and the things we don't, the people regarded as role models, and so on, are ways in which learning is reflected in culture. The socialisation of new recruits involves their picking up these soft elements of culture as well as the hard elements of routines and processes.

The fourth way – and perhaps the most obvious, though not necessarily the most useful way – that organisations store knowledge is to record it in reports, databases, and so on. Just because something is recorded doesn't mean that it can easily be accessed and retrieved – how many reports gather dust while someone reinvents the wheel?

Storing and retrieving knowledge effectively is the challenge for knowledge management. My own view is that the key to knowledge management in many contexts is more about relationships and communication between people than it is about systems and databases.

Creating a learning organisation or team: a systematic approach

If you want your own team to function as a learning organisation, then you need to help them to systematically review their performance and to figure out how they want to do things differently. The Coverdale systematic approach is a very practical way to translate this notion of a learning organisation into reality.

Ralph Coverdale set up the Coverdale Organisation in 1965 to offer programmes and consultancy to help individuals, teams and organisations to carry out their work in ways that are both more productive and more fulfilling. At the heart of the Coverdale method is a systematic approach to getting things done, either as an individual or in a group.

There are three stages in any task – *preparation*, *action* and *review.*

In the *preparation* stage the starting point is to become very clear about the *aims*. Clarifying aims translates into crisp statements of purpose (*why are we doing this?*), deliverables and measures of success.

Having established aims, there are three activities in *planning* a piece of work – gathering information, deciding what has to be done (WHTBD), and making detailed plans.

The *action* stage involves carrying out the detailed plan, which may of course need to be modified as events unfold.

The *review* stage involves asking questions in two areas. The first concerns the results – *Did we achieve what we set out to do? How could the result be improved?* etc. The second concerns the process of how the task was done – *What went well that we can use next time? What were the difficulties and how can we avoid them next time?* etc.

Figure 5.1 summarises the systematic approach.

Figure 5.1   The Coverdale systematic approach

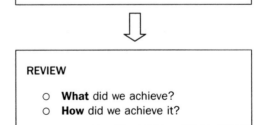

PREPARATION

AIMS

- O   What is the purpose of the task?
- O   What is the desired end product?
- O   How will we recognise success?

PLANNING

- O   Information
- O   What has to be done? (WHTBD)
- O   Action plan

ACTION

- O   Carry out the plans
- O   Modify as necessary

REVIEW

- O   **What** did we achieve?
- O   **How** did we achieve it?

In his book *Coverdale on Management*, Max Taylor explains how the systematic approach becomes a learning method:

> Experience by itself may teach very little: improvements only come from reviewing what happened, understanding why, and pulling out the lessons that one can use for the future. If the review is carried out consciously and deliberately, the learning will come faster. This is indeed the basic way in which skill (as opposed to knowledge) is learnt – by a cycle of *thought – action – thought,* which corresponds with *preparation – action – review.* Ten minutes' review at the end of a job or at the end of a day can save many hours for the future; it makes sure that one actually learns from experience – which is not something which nature provides on her own, or there would be fewer old fools in the world. (Taylor, 1979)

The learning which is distilled in a Coverdale review session is mainly inductive – that is, groups draw out lessons from what actually happened and identify what they will do in the future. The reviews focus more on what went well because a group which has done something once can repeat it. If something has gone badly, the group notes this and works out what they will do differently next time. Thus the reviews lead to practical ideas to be tried out in action. The emphasis on the positive and the constructive also boosts morale.

The Coverdale approach offers benefits at individual, team and organisational levels. One person can use the ideas on a piece of individual work, or to help a group be more effective even when no one else is aware of the approach. The methods are even more powerful when used to tackle tasks collectively, giving a group a common framework and language to plan and execute work, to measure success, and to review and learn.

The greatest impact comes when it is adopted across an organisation, with genuine commitment and active involvement from the top. For example, John Harvey Jones introduced the Coverdale approach to 'unite the management' from seven separate divisions on ICI's huge petrochemical complex on Teesside. In *Making It Happen* he writes:

> The outcome and output of the course consisted of a number of important lessons, and I guess each one of us who attended it took away rather different things. First, I gained an understanding of the importance of process, and process planning, second a realization that listening is an art and a skill and needs to be developed, and third an understanding that almost invariably businessmen seek to go into action far too early – before they have actually discussed, analysed, and decided what they are going to do. (Harvey Jones, 1988)

If you were to ask me how you could transform your department or company into a learning organisation, I would suggest that you consider the Coverdale approach.

Creating relationships

All real living is meeting. (Martin Buber)

Introduction

In this chapter I invite you to reflect on the nature of the relationships you have with those who work for you. I suggest three different but overlapping ways in which you might think about these relationships:

- What are the metaphors that you use – implicitly or explicitly – when you think, speak and act as a manager?

- What is the typical nature of the interactions between you and the members of the team that you lead?

- How much emotional intelligence do you demonstrate in managing your relationships with other people?

In earlier chapters I put forward definitions of coaching and mentoring that began by emphasising that these are *relationships*. Whether you want to or not, as a manager you inevitably have a relationship with each of the people who work for you. The nature of these relationships may be close or distant, supportive or uncooperative, productive or dysfunctional. You may think deeply about your relationships or be blissfully unaware of their character.

Whatever the case, the relationships exist and influence the effectiveness of you and your team.

Images of organisation

Alison Hardingham writes that, 'The meaning that any event has depends upon the "frame" in which we perceive it. When we change the frame, we change the meaning'.

As human beings, we use language to think about and talk about our world. The language we use shapes the frames through which we view the world. And how we see the world affects how we behave and the actions we take.

As an illustration, the US president George W. Bush has declared a 'war on terrorism'. Defining the situation as a 'war' suggests other forms of language and action – enemy, attack, bomb, assault, defend, protect, and so on – associated with a state of war between nations. A 'mission against terrorism' might conjure somewhat different associations and actions. Note that I am not intending to make any political point whatsoever here – I'm merely trying to illustrate the power of language to shape how we see things and, therefore, how we act.

In using language to describe and think about our world we draw on metaphors. A metaphor uses words in a way that is not literal. A metaphor is simply a way of conceiving of something, a perspective on it.

Any metaphor offers a partial way of looking at something. Like looking at a mountain from different sides, different metaphors offer different perspectives. To say that a man is a lion suggests that he is brave and strong, but not that he has four legs and is covered in fur. Thus any metaphor is incomplete, and potentially misleading.

A metaphor is neither true nor false. Rather, the usefulness of a metaphor depends on the richness of the insights it generates.

In *Images of Organisation*, Gareth Morgan explores a variety of metaphors for making sense of organisations. He writes that, 'The use of metaphor implies a way of thinking and a way of seeing that pervade how we understand our world generally'.

Morgan adds that his book, 'is based on a very simple premise: that all theories of organization and management are based on implicit images or metaphors that lead us to see, understand, and manage organizations in distinctive yet partial ways'.

By far the most common metaphor used to think about organisations is the notion of the organisation as a *machine*. In this metaphor the organisation is viewed as made up of interlocking parts that fit together. When we draw a typical organisation chart, with a hierarchy of roles and reporting relationships, we are – generally unconsciously – using a machine metaphor of the organisation. The machine metaphor is so deeply ingrained that many of us don't realise that we are using it or that there may be other ways of thinking about organisations.

When we speak of improving efficiency, raising productivity, driving change, re-engineering, devolving responsibility or cascading objectives, we are using the machine metaphor.

Morgan writes that:

> The whole thrust of classical management theory and its modern application is to suggest that organizations can or should be rational systems that operate in as efficient a manner as possible. While many will endorse this as an ideal, it is easier said than done, because we are dealing with people, not inanimate cogs and wheels. (Morgan, 1996)

Morgan points out that the machine metaphor works well under conditions where machines work well. These conditions include a stable environment and where the human parts are compliant and well behaved. A mechanistic approach to organisations works less well when circumstances change. Thus in times of environmental change and internal reorganisation, the machine metaphor has limitations and may even – as any metaphor can – be misleading.

Morgan then goes on to consider the metaphor that sees organisations as organisms – that is, as living systems existing in a wider environment and needing to adapt to changes in that environment. The organism metaphor has been widely employed over the last 50 years, and we are using it when we talk about corporate survival, product lifecycles or organisational health checks. A SWOT analysis of your organisation's strengths and weaknesses and the opportunities and threats in its business environment is based on this metaphor.

Morgan introduces the organism metaphor by talking about different species of organisation in different environments:

> Just as we find polar bears in arctic regions, camels in deserts, and alligators in swamps, we notice that certain species of organization are better 'adapted' to specific environmental conditions than others. We find bureaucratic organizations tend to work most effectively in environments that are stable or protected in some way and that very different species are found in more competitive and turbulent regions, such as the environments of high-tech firms in the aerospace and micro-electronics industries. (Morgan, 1996)

Morgan also explores the implications of other ways of looking at organisations – for example, as brains, as cultures, as political systems, and as psychic prisons. Each of these metaphors offers insights into how organisations work and how they might be more effective.

Images of manager

What then is the metaphor or metaphors that frame – perhaps unconsciously – how you think about your role as a manager of people?

In classical management theory, the manager's role is to plan, organise, monitor and control work. There is a chain of command from the top to the bottom of the organisation. More modern versions of this emphasise management by objectives and sophisticated management information systems.

This view of management is based on the *machine* metaphor of an organisation. It prompts language such as superiors and subordinates, being in charge, supervising. Much of the language arises from military settings – chain of command, front-line staff, strategy (which comes from the Greek word meaning a general). In fact, in the first half of the twentieth century, the military principles worked out by Frederick the Great and others became the foundation of both classical management theory and the machine metaphor for describing organisations.

This perspective – which I shall refer to as the *control* metaphor of management – is as deeply ingrained in everyday thinking as the *machine* metaphor of organisation. Like the machine metaphor, the control metaphor works well when the environment is stable and the human parts are compliant. It is limiting, however, in times of change or complexity.

Another more recent metaphor for management is the idea first set out by Robert Greenleaf on servant-leadership. In this view of leadership, the manager's first task is to serve their people.

A simple illustration of servant-leadership is seen in the inverted organisation chart which puts the people who deal with the organisation's customers at the top of the chart, those who manage these people below, and senior management at the bottom of the chart supporting everyone else.

Both the *control* and the *servant* metaphors can be applied within a hierarchical organisation structure. Peter Senge makes a thought-provoking point, 'Only when the choice to serve undergirds the moral formation of leaders does the hierarchical power that separates the leader and those led not corrupt'.

The title of this book is *Growing People*. This contains within it the notion that your role as a manager is to grow and nurture the people who work for you. The metaphor suggests that as a manager you are a *gardener* or perhaps a *farmer*. As a gardener, you need to provide the conditions in which people can flourish – perhaps you need to give them space, or sow the seed of an idea. It implies that your people have potential to develop, change and evolve. Other ideas that might flow from this metaphor are that you may need to get rid of dead wood, weed some people out and create headroom for others. As a metaphor it is inevitably partial and may be misleading. For example, it may suggest that you are a different species from those who work for you – you are an agent who does things to a lesser order of species. On reflection, this is perhaps exactly how some managers see things.

Each of these metaphors – commander or servant or gardener – offers a frame for thinking about your role as a manager and your relationships with the people who work for you. Each can illuminate some aspects of your role and each can mislead. You may wish to explore how you typically view your role as a manager and consider the metaphors that are implicit in the way you relate to those who work for you. Perhaps there is another metaphor – another image of manager – that makes more sense for you?

Adult:adult relationships

Another way of looking at relationships is through transactional analysis (TA). This is a psychological theory that offers a simple but powerful way to consider the nature of the interactions between people.

TA describes three mental states that each of us switch between – parent, adult and child.

- The *adult* me is mature, rational, emotionally intelligent, and focused on solving problems.
- The *parent* me wants to look after people, often in a controlling way but sometimes in a nurturing way.
- The *child* me is dominated by my feelings, often fearful, inhibited and hesitant, but sometimes playful, creative and energetic.

In *I'm OK – You're OK*, Thomas Harris writes:

Continual observation has supported the assumption that these three states exist in all people. It is as if in each person there is the same little person he was when he was three years old. There are also within him his own parents. These are recordings in the brain of actual experiences of internal and external events, the most significant of which happened during the first five years of life. There is a third state, different from these two. The first two are called Parent and Child, and the third, Adult. (Harris, 1974)

All of us spend time in each of these mental states. When we change from one state to another it becomes apparent in our words, gestures, manner, appearance and even bodily function. Next time you catch yourself wagging a finger at someone and telling them what they really should have done, I'll wager you've slipped into your critical parent state. This state often triggers the adapted child in the other person, and you end up with a series of parent:child transactions.

Many of the interactions between a superior and a subordinate in a hierarchical organisation are of the parent:child variety. When this becomes the norm – perhaps an unspoken or implicit norm – it is then a central feature of the culture of the organisation. This may be very effective – it is, for example, the basis of military discipline. And it may suit all parties. It gives superiors a sense of power, control, status and prestige. It offers subordinates a sense that their role is to follow orders or instructions, which can be quite comfortable.

A culture based on parent:child interactions between managers and staff simplifies and structures life. It lets subordinates save their creativity and their passion for activities outside work. It means, however, that the organisation draws on a mere fraction of the talent and potential of its people. In turn, they miss opportunities to contribute more, gain greater job satisfaction and realise their potential.

An alternative is to seek to establish a culture within your team based on adult:adult interactions. This will require you to be straight in your dealings with people, to be open and honest, to see others as your equal (even though you may be more experienced or talented), to demonstrate appropriate levels of trust in those you manage, and in fact to trust yourself to let go some of the mechanisms of control.

This is not a prescription for naivety. You may, for example, be managing inexperienced staff who need clear direction. Or you may be working in an environment with a history of mistrust or where relationships between management and staff are very much seen as 'us and them'. You need to start from where you are, and changing this kind of culture may be a very long journey indeed.

The philosophy behind a coaching approach to management suggests that a culture based on adult:adult interactions will achieve better results and will build people's capability for the future. It views people as having within themselves talent and potential that you as a manager coach can encourage. Similarly, if you see your role as being there to serve or to grow the people on your team, helping them to maximise their contribution and fulfil their potential, you will create more adult:adult interactions. You can aim, over time, to establish this as the norm and the culture within your team.

The benefits from establishing a culture where relationships are open, honest and straight and based on adult:adult interactions are far-reaching:

- people will bring more of their enthusiasm, energy and talent to work;

- people will deliver more and gain greater job satisfaction;

- people will build their capability by taking on bigger challenges;

- people's self image will grow as they see themselves contributing more, achieving more and being valued more;

- the performance of the organisation will improve;

- the capability of the organisation will grow;

- morale will be enhanced;

- stress will be reduced;

- people will feel better about the organisation as an employer, making it more likely that they will want to remain in the organisation and making it easier for the organisation to attract new employees.

In *Turning to One Another* Meg Wheatley writes that:

> Conversation can only take place among equals. If anyone feels superior, it destroys conversation. Words are then used to dominate, coerce. Those who act superior can't help but treat others as objects to accomplish their causes and plans. When we see each other as equals, we stop misusing them. We are equal because we are human beings. Acknowledging you as my equal is a gesture of love. (Wheatley, 2002)

You may wish to consider in what ways you consider yourself superior to those that you manage.

Emotional intelligence

Another way of thinking about creating effective relationships is through the notion of emotional intelligence. The term emotional intelligence – or EI – is currently much in vogue. Daniel Goleman, whose writings popularised the

Figure 6.1   Emotional intelligence

	Awareness	Management
Others	*Empathy*	*Social skills*
Self	*Self awareness*	*Self control*

term, begins his book *Emotional Intelligence* with a quote from Aristotle which captures the essence of EI:

> Anyone can become angry – that is easy. But to be angry with the right person, to the right degree, at the right time, for the right purpose, and in the right way – that is not easy.

The framework in Figure 6.1 offers a simple but useful way of thinking about emotional intelligence.

As the figure suggests, emotional intelligence means, first of all, being aware of your own feelings and the feelings of others and then, second, being able to manage your own feelings effectively and to manage your relationships with others successfully.

At the heart of both emotional intelligence and of effective leadership lies self awareness. Understanding yourself is fundamental. In *The Emotional Intelligence Pocketbook,* Margaret Chapman writes:

> Self-awareness is the ability to see ourselves with our own eyes, to be aware of our ...

- Goals, immediate and long-term

- Beliefs, about ourselves and others

- Values, those things we hold dear

- Drivers, that affect how we work
- Rules, that we live by, the *shoulds, musts* and *oughts*
- Self-talk, the inner voice that tells us we *can* or *cannot* do something

… and the ways in which these impact on what we do and contribute to our *map of the world.* (Chapman, 2001)

To develop your emotional intelligence and to bring into focus what underpins your approach to managing people, you will find it very useful to spend some time – on your own or with someone you trust – clarifying and articulating your goals, beliefs, values, drivers, rules and self-talk.

An emotionally intelligent leader can achieve far more through their team than one who can only work at a task level. Emotionally intelligent managers are able to empathise, communicate, build relationships and establish consensus. They understand what makes people tick and can use this constructively to manage performance and to develop capability. Daniel Goleman estimates that for leadership positions, emotional intelligence competencies account for up to 85 per cent of what sets outstanding managers apart from the average. A survey of managers in a UK supermarket chain found that those with high EI experienced less stress, enjoyed better health, performed better and reported a better work/life balance. There are wide reaching benefits – both for yourself and for those you manage – in being more emotionally intelligent.

Developing your emotional intelligence

Whereas conventional intelligence – as measured by IQ – is more or less given, you can improve your emotional intelligence as you go through life. Your life experiences – and how you handle them – will be a far richer source of emotional development than any book or course.

Here are some ways in which you might use your day-to-day experiences to develop the various aspects of emotional intelligence.

- Learn to recognise and put a name to your feelings. Use three word sentences that begin 'I feel ...' – for example, I feel happy or I feel angry. (Note – a sentence which begins 'I feel that ...' generally indicates a thought, not an emotion.)

- The term 'self talk' refers to the things that we say to ourselves – inside our head, as it were. Think about the messages you are saying to yourself. Consider how your self talk might be shaping your behaviour. What would be more useful self talk?

- Keep a journal that records significant events where you felt strongly about something or someone. Make a note of how you felt, what you thought, what you said or did (or what you didn't say or do), and what the consequences were. From time to time look back at your journal and see if there are any patterns.

- Note what happens next time you are in a conflict situation. Do you passively withdraw or give up? Do you aggressively seek to win at the expense of the other party? Or do you assertively look for how both of you can gain some benefit – a win-win outcome?

- Spend some time clarifying what really matters to you in your life.

- Observe those people who create positive, nourishing relationships with others. What can you learn from how they treat people?

- Observe those people who leave you feeling drained or upset or somehow less positive. What do they do that triggers this? How do you collude with them?

- Who are the key people that you interact with at work and outside work? What really matters to each of these people? What can you do to make your relationships with each of them more satisfying and productive?

- Practise empathy – develop your active listening skills and try to pick up on the emotions as well as the facts. Explore the things that are important but are not being said.

7

Conversations that make a difference

The core act of leadership must be the act of making conversations real. (David Whyte)

Introduction

In the previous chapter we looked in various ways at the nature of your relationships with those who work for you. You fashion these relationships day by day through the conversations you have – or fail to have – with people. In this chapter I want to look more closely at how you can create conversations that get to the heart of the matter – conversations that make a difference for you and your team. In particular we shall contrast *debate* with *dialogue*, and look at the skills you need to engage in dialogue.

From time to time in your relationships – both at work and outside – you will need to have conversations that are difficult. We shall look at what makes conversations difficult, and then consider how you might position these as learning conversations to make them more productive – and less difficult.

Conversations create relationships. This is not to deny, however, that actions always speak louder than words. If you make promises to your people that you don't keep – or if you fail your team when the chips are down – you'll damage your relationships, perhaps fatally.

From debate to dialogue

Debate is something we are all familiar with. We hear it in Parliament, in our adversarial legal system, and in disputes between management and trade unions. Debate assumes that there is a single right answer – generally one's own – and that the goal is to find this answer or to win the argument. Debate is about winning or losing, or perhaps compromising.

Dialogue is much less common. Dialogue assumes that there are multiple perspectives, and the goal is to explore these different viewpoints in order to understand each other's position. It is about exploring ideas together, generating fresh insights and creating new possibilities. Dialogue is about searching creatively for win-win outcomes.

Many commercial negotiations are conducted as a debate, where each side is trying to score over the other. But commercial negotiations can be conducted in the spirit of seeking an agreement where both parties win. This is often the key to successful long-term commercial partnerships.

Participants in a debate take a critical stance, looking for the flaws in the other argument. They listen in order to challenge, and they interrogate rather than inquire. There are times when this is appropriate – for example, the progress of scientific and academic thought is based on intellectual debate, scrutiny of evidence and analysis of arguments.

On the other hand, participants in a dialogue are curious about each other's views, looking for what is new or what they can learn. They listen in order to understand, and they inquire to deepen their understanding.

You might like to reflect on the nature of the conversations in your team meetings or your other encounters with colleagues or clients. How often are you seeking to impose your view? How often are you seeking to build a shared understanding from which can emerge a new way forward?

There are three skills which are required to engage effectively in dialogue – listening, inquiring and voicing. Let's look at these in turn.

Listening

In *Dialogue and the Art of Thinking Together*, Bill Isaacs says that 'The heart of dialogue is a simple but profound capacity to listen'.

We have already noted that listening is one of the key skills you need to coach effectively. Listening well is important to understand the other person's point of view, and it helps you to frame the questions that will prompt them to think.

The words that people say may be only the tip of the iceberg. The feelings that lie beneath the words are often expressed non-verbally. To be a really effective listener you need to tune into what is not being said. Gina Hayden uses the notion of an iceberg to illustrate different levels of listening (Figure 7.1)

You need to listen with your heart and your intuition to hear the messages that are there but not spoken. Sometimes your gut tells you things well before your intellect catches on.

Good listening, however, does more than enable you to understand the other person – it builds the relationship. Meg Wheatley writes:

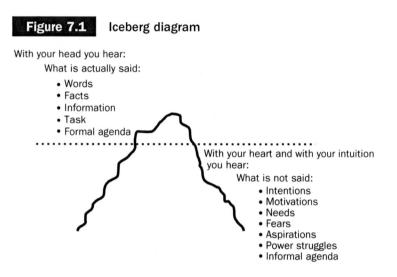

Figure 7.1 Iceberg diagram

With your head you hear:
What is actually said:
- Words
- Facts
- Information
- Task
- Formal agenda

With your heart and with your intuition you hear:
What is not said:
- Intentions
- Motivations
- Needs
- Fears
- Aspirations
- Power struggles
- Informal agenda

One of the easiest human acts is also the most healing. Listening to someone. Simply listening. Not advising or coaching, but silently and fully listening. Why is being heard so healing? I don't know the full answer to that question, but I do know that it has something to do with the fact that listening creates relationship. (Wheatley, 2002)

There is a further dimension to listening that is important in dialogue – listening to yourself. This means listening to the voice inside your head for your assumptions and your judgments. When you notice a strong reaction in yourself to what someone says, it is worth checking internally to see if one of your deeply held views is being threatened or if some episode from your past has echoes in the present conversation.

Inquiring

Susan Scott illustrates how we all see the world differently with the notion of *beach ball reality*. Think of your organisation as a beach ball which has four big coloured stripes – say, blue, red, yellow and green. If you live every day on the blue stripe then the world looks blue to you. If I spend all my time on the red stripe, then I see the world as red. Rather than engage in a debate about whether the world is blue or red, it is more useful to recognise that each perspective is valid and that the world is blue from one perspective and red from another. When we inquire together into how we each see the world, we develop a far richer understanding of reality and its complexity.

When you engage in a debate kind of conversation, you use questions to find flaws in the other person's argument or to find evidence to support your own position. You might ask questions when you already have an answer in mind, to lead the other person to your view.

In dialogue, however, you ask questions to explore together with other people the different perspectives that are in the room, including your own. You can also use questions to bring to the surface the thinking and assumptions that lie behind your own and other people's positions. By sharing perspectives and surfacing assumptions you begin to create new possibilities that respect the views and needs of everyone involved. A stance of non-judgmental acceptance is crucial. Remember that seeking to understand fully someone's views does not imply that you agree with them.

When inquiring it is very helpful to have an attitude of genuine curiosity and openness. Meg Wheatley writes:

> When I'm in conversation, I try to maintain curiosity by reminding myself that everyone here has something to teach me. When they're saying things I disagree with, or have never thought about, or that I consider foolish or wrong, I silently remind myself that they have something to teach me. Somehow this little

reminder helps me to be more attentive and less judgmental. It helps me to stay open to people, rather than shut them out. (Wheatley, 2002)

In conversation the opposite of curiosity is certainty. When you are certain you understand the other person's point of view, you stop inquiring and you probably also stop listening.

Ladder of inference

Human beings think very quickly. We have the capacity to assess a situation and come to a conclusion in an instant. Because we arrive at our conclusions so readily, and the wisdom of our viewpoint seems so obvious to us, we think it must be just as apparent to others. Consequently, when faced with a difference of opinion, we tend to throw our conclusions back and forth at each another, leaving the conversation to go around in circles while we argue about the facts and details.

This can be illustrated as a a ladder of inference (Figure 7.2), a notion developed by Chris Argyris and popularised by Peter Senge. From the pool of available data, we choose that which suits our case, we make interpretations about what the data means, and we draw conclusions. We then swap 'information' at the level of these conclusions. I may be so familiar and comfortable with an opinion that I offer it as the truth and cannot understand why you don't see things as I do.

Next time you find yourself in a discussion that is going round in circles, trading opinions without making any progress, you might try to move the conversation into inquiry mode by walking down the ladder of inference with the other participants. To do this, you need to:

Figure 7.2   Ladder of inference

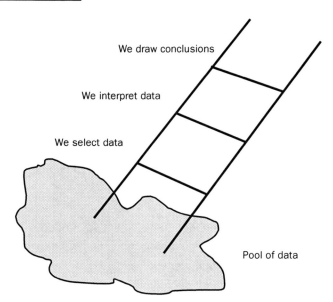

- suspend judgment;
- recognise that different perspectives are valid;
- become curious about other points of view;
- articulate assumptions and values;
- seek to create new understandings and ways forward.

Voicing

The third skill required to engage in meaningful dialogue is *voicing* – the ability to state clearly what you think and the reasons that underlie your thinking.

There is a place for small talk and polite conversation. When you meet someone for the first time at a party, for example, it is normal to talk about your journey or the weather or how you know the host. Such small talk may be the first step to a much more meaningful level of engagement.

It is important in dialogue to go beyond polite talk and speak authentically. In *Difficult Conversations*, Douglas Stone, Bruce Patton and Sheila Heen write that,

> When we fail to share what's important to us, we detach ourselves from others and damage our relationships... A relationship takes hold and grows when both participants experience themselves and the other as being authentic. (Stone et al., 1999)

In dialogue it is important not merely to state your point of view but also to reveal the thinking that led you to it. Misunderstandings can arise when you simply swap conclusions at the top of your ladder of inference. It is important to share where your conclusions come from and to avoid presenting opinions as fact.

When voicing what is true for you it is worth checking what your intent is. If, for example, your intention is to blame or to dump a load of negative feelings or to get someone to change, you probably need to pause and find the words that will convey what you really need to say without attacking the other.

It is also important to invite others to speak with their authentic voice, asking them to share how they see things and what leads them to see them in that way.

Some people find it very difficult to say what is true for them. Indeed at a deeper, psychological level they may believe that they are not entitled to express their views and feelings. In your own team there may be some people who struggle to say what they really think or feel. This might be because they are young and inexperienced, and simply need some encouragement to come forward with their views. Or, it might be because of a deeper lack of assertiveness which prohibits them from speaking authentically or asking for what they want. One of your challenges as a manager is to work out how best to converse with each individual.

Panel 7.1: Thinking rounds and validated listening

Here are two exercises used by Gina Hayden and her colleagues that you might use with your team to give everyone a chance to speak up and have their views heard. The exercises are deliberately designed to slow down the conversation and encourage people to listen to one another and to think.

Thinking rounds

Begin by identifying clearly the topic for discussion – it probably helps to have this written down where everyone can see it.

Each person, in turn, states their views, thoughts, ideas or experiences regarding this question for one minute, uninterrupted by others.

This is followed by a second round, where each person has one minute to build on the thinking shared during round one (again, without interruption or discussion).

A final round follows, where each person has one minute to state what they believe is the best thinking generated by the group.

Summarise and flipchart the best thinking from the group on the topic.

As well as slowing down the conversation, this structure encourages a number of other things. It gives everyone a

---

chance to speak, with equal air time, which can be particularly useful in a hierarchical group. It also prompts participants to listen to each other as interrupting is ruled out. Finally, it encourages everyone to build on each other's ideas. The outcome generated is a team effort.

Validated listening

Each person gets one minute to voice their views, but the next person to speak first has to summarise the views of the previous speaker to the satisfaction of that person before voicing their own views. This is another useful way of slowing down the conversation and getting team members to really listen to each other. It gives an experience of listening fully rather than switching off in order to 'reload' one's next comments or views. It also enables each person to be listened to with equal merit.

Silence

Many years ago I took a Certificate in Counselling. One of the tutors, George Henshaw, offered us a motto at the beginning of the course: *Don't just do something, sit there.* Over the years I have found this a tremendously useful guide when coaching or counselling, helping me to wait till the other person is ready to speak.

In dialogue, silence achieves a number of purposes. It gives everyone in the room a chance to participate. It gives all involved a chance to think about what has been said, and to reflect on beliefs or assumptions. It gives people time to identify what to say next or to consider what actions might be required.

One of Susan Scott's seven principles of *Fierce Conversations* is: *Let the silence do the heavy lifting.* She writes that:

> During my conversations with the people most important to me, silence has become my favorite sound, because that is when the work is being done. Of all the tools I use during conversations and all the principles I keep in mind, silence is the most powerful of all. (Scott, 2002)

She draws a comparison with the intervals between the notes in a piece of music, the phrasing that gives it magic, 'When we are completely engaged in talking, all of the possibilities for the conversation grow smaller'.

Debate and dialogue

Gina Hayden summarises the differences between debate and dialogue in Table 7.1 (based on Deborah Flick's book *From Debate to Dialogue*).

Table 7.1   Differences between debate and dialogue

	Debate	Dialogue
Premise	In any given situation there is only one right answer or right perspective, usually one's own	In any given situation there are multiple valid answers and perspectives, including one's own
Goal	To win, to be right, to sell, persuade or convince To find the right answer	To understand the other person from within their own point of view and explore the different viewpoints (To understand *does not mean* necessarily to agree)
Attitude	Evaluative and critical, looking for gaps	Curious and open, seeking new understanding

Table 7.1 Differences between debate and dialogue (*cont'd*)

	Debate	Dialogue
Focus	What's wrong with this picture?	What's new? Of value? What can I learn?
Listening	Accept little at face value Listen to challenge others' views Listen critically for errors or flawed logic Apply judgment Talk more than you listen Plan your rebuttal – wait to talk	Accept what is said at face value as true for others Hear others' views as a chance to deepen understanding of them Listen for their story Suspend judgment Listen more than you talk – allow silence Reflect instead of react – allow the conversation to evolve
Inquiring	Interrogate the other person and their views Ask questions that support your perspective and challenge the other person's perspective	Ask questions to understand more about the other person's views Explore assumptions – yours and others'
Voicing	Assert and justify your position Describe gaps in the other person's thinking Defend your assumptions as being the truth Say what you think is expected – speak from role	Describe your reality and invite others to describe theirs Speak with your authentic voice – your true thoughts Acknowledge feelings where appropriate Acknowledge your contribution to the situation

Conversations that get to the heart of the matter, that surface assumptions and explore different perspectives take time. They might seem like an indulgence in today's fast-paced organisations. However, the conversations that don't get to the heart of the matter ultimately take up far more time because the decisions and actions 'agreed' in these conversations don't address the full reality of the situation.

As Susan Scott says, 'fierce conversations often do take time. The problem is, anything else takes longer'.

Meg Wheatley explains why we need to make time if we want to engage in conversations like these. She says that we need to slow down the conversation to a pace that encourages thinking. We need to slow down to give us time to get to know each other. Thinking is not inaction. 'Thinking is the place where intelligent action begins', she writes.

Difficult conversations

From time to time as a manager you will need to have a difficult conversation with one of your people or with your team about, for example, underperformance or unacceptable behaviour. In *Difficult Conversations*, Stone et al. set out a framework to understand and to manage the difficult conversations we all face from time to time at work or outside. A difficult conversation, they say, is anything you find it hard to talk about.

Their starting point is that any difficult conversation is actually three conversations:

- *The 'what happened?' conversation.* Most difficult conversations involve disagreements about what has happened or what should happen.

- *The feelings conversation.* Every difficult conversation also asks and answers questions about feelings. These feelings may not be addressed directly, but they will leak in anyway.

- *The identity conversation.* This is the conversation we each have with ourselves about what this situation means to us.

To illustrate these three conversations, imagine that you are talking to one of your staff about how they failed to deliver an important piece of work to the quality that was required. What might be going on for both of you during this conversation?

First, there is the *what happened?* conversation. This might cover issues such as how clear was your briefing, how realistic was the timetable, what resources were available, what else happened to interrupt the work, and so on.

Second, there is the *feelings* conversation. This might never be articulated and one or both of you may not be conscious of your feelings. Nevertheless, those feelings will still be there. For example, you may feel disappointed or angry because you think they let you down. They may be upset because they think you failed to provide adequate support. The nature of the relationship between you will influence how much these feelings are explored.

Third, there is the *identity* conversation. This is probably even less likely to be voiced. Perhaps part of your identity is to see yourself as a competent manager who gives all of your staff a lot of support. On this occasion you didn't give enough support, and this raises questions in your mind about how good a manager you really are. Equally the other person sees themselves as a conscientious and reliable worker, and this episode may cause them to question just how dependable they really are. Again the quality of the relationship between you will affect how far this conversation takes place. Even if nothing is said, each of you may be having part of this conversation in your own head.

There are three identity issues that are particularly common and underlie many difficult conversations:

- Am I competent?
- Am I a good person?
- Am I worthy of love?

Alison Hardingham suggests three liberating answers to these questions:

- I am competent but not perfect.
- I am good but not a saint.
- I am worthy of love but not loved by everyone.

Tackling difficult conversations

Stone et al. (1999) suggest that one way of engaging effectively in a difficult conversation is to move to a *learning* conversation.

A difficult conversation is typically like a debate, as we have been describing it. You are trying to prove a point, or tell someone what you think about them, or get them to do something. You are in a form of 'message delivery' mode. This is likely to be met by some kind of resistance, and you probably end up in a conflict and a win-lose situation where even to 'win' might only be of short-term benefit.

Shifting to a mindset of engaging in a *learning* conversation means that your purpose changes and you want to share and understand different perspectives, explore feelings and possibly questions of identity, and look to construct positive ways forward that will benefit all parties. Shifting from *message delivery* to *learning* means that you stop arguing about who is right and start exploring each other's stories. This is like moving from debate to dialogue.

An important key to having a learning conversation is to distinguish blame from contribution. Rather than arguing about who is to blame, it is far more fruitful to explore what each of us contributed to the situation. Some of the differences in moving from blame to contribution are summarised in Table 7.2.

Table 7.2	Distinguishing blame from contribution

Who is to blame?	What is my contribution?
Seeks to judge others	Seeks to understand others
One sided	Joint and interactive
Looks backwards	Looks forwards
Provokes defensiveness	Stimulates learning and change
Hinders problem solving	Encourages problem solving

Stone et al. write that:

> Talking about blame distracts us from exploring why things went wrong and how we might correct them going forward. Focusing instead on understanding the contribution system allows us to learn about the real causes of the problem, and to work on correcting them. The distinction between blame and contribution may seem subtle. But it is a distinction worth working to understand, because it will make a significant difference in your ability to handle difficult conversations. (Stone et al., 1999)

Making sense of conversations

David Kantor offers a couple of frameworks that you may find useful in making sense of some of the conversations that you have with your team or, more generally, as you talk with other people.

He suggests that people use three different languages to express themselves – power, meaning and affect (or feeling).

- Someone who is using the language of *power* is interested in what we are going to do.

- Someone who is using the language of *meaning* is interested in the ideas and values behind what is happening.

- Someone who is using the language of *affect* is concerned about the feelings of the people involved and the relationships between them.

Bill Isaacs writes that:

> These are in fact truly different languages: Communication across them carries the same difficulties that translation between any two languages carries. People speaking the language of feeling tend to be discounted by people who speak the language of action and power. Asking such people to reflect about the meaning of things can often evoke the reaction that you are being too 'intellectual'. And asking questions about how to take action may feel premature to those communicating via the language of feeling or meaning. (Isaacs, 1999)

You may like to reflect on which of the three languages is your 'native tongue', the one that you typically use. Which people on your team naturally use a different language? What might you do to understand each other more fully?

The second framework is Kantor's four player system. This describes four stances that people take in a conversation (Figure 7.3):

- When someone *moves*, they are proposing something or initiating an action.

- When someone *follows*, they are supporting a move.

- When someone *opposes*, they are challenging what is being said or proposed.

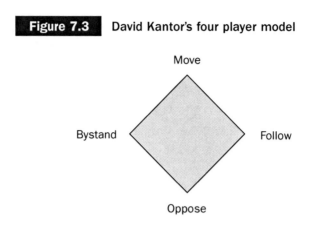

Figure 7.3 David Kantor's four player model

Move

Bystand

Follow

Oppose

- When someone *bystands*, they are offering a perspective on what is happening in the conversation. (Note that the term bystanding does not mean being uninvolved or silent.)

Kantor argues that a healthy conversation requires all of these roles to be played. Moreover, everyone in the conversation is free to occupy any of the four positions.

You might like to think about your own strengths and weaknesses in conversations. What roles do you play particularly well or not so well? What roles do you habitually occupy or, on the other hand, never take?

Similarly, consider the conversations that take place in your team meetings. How easy is it for others to make a move, or to oppose you? Who follows you unquestioningly, and whose support depends on whether your move seems sensible or not? Who plays a bystanding role and offers a comment or question about the dynamics of the conversation?

8

Talent management

Who gets what job: the heart of development. (Morgan McCall)

Introduction

In this final chapter I want to shift the focus somewhat. In previous chapters we have mainly been looking at your role as a manager supporting the development of the people who work for you. In the final chapter I shall set out some ideas on how you and your colleagues on a management team can collectively identify and nurture the talented people within your organisation or department.

I shall call this process *talent management*. The key notion underpinning this book – that real learning requires real experience together with reflection to make sense of that experience – also provides the essential foundation for talent management.

You will see this described elsewhere as *succession management* or *succession planning*. There are subtle differences in emphasis in using the term *talent* rather than *succession*. For me, *succession* has a sense of looking to find people who can fill boxes on organisation charts, whereas *talent* suggests a more dynamic process focused on the potential of individuals rather than the roles they might fill.

On the other hand, for some people the word *talent* may have connotations of elitism and perhaps a disregard for the majority of people in the organisation. I also prefer the word *management* to *planning* in this context. *Talent management* or *succession management* sounds like a more complete process leading to action than simply *succession planning*.

Overview of talent management

In the next few pages I'd like to build up a diagram showing the elements that together make up a strategy to identify and manage talent proactively and effectively. The rest of the chapter will fill out these elements in more detail.

The aim in talent management is simply to identify the people in the organisation who have more talent than others and then to develop these people so that they become more experienced and competent, able to play a greater part in the success of the organisation (Figure 8.1). Note that in focusing extra effort on those with more talent you are still looking at the same time to develop all of your people.

Stage one: what defines talent?

I believe it is very important that you and your colleagues on the management team articulate what you mean by talent – what are the qualities or behaviours that make someone in your eyes more talented than their contemporaries? Otherwise, you run the risk of making poor assessments, with a danger that *talented* may implicitly equate to *someone like us*.

Figure 8.1   The aim of talent management

Talented individuals → More capable individuals

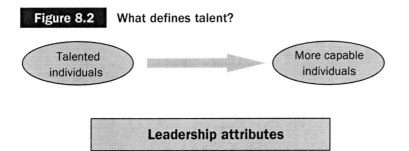

Figure 8.2 What defines talent?

In this chapter I am assuming that you are looking to develop the future leaders of your organisation. You may be in a role where technical ability is important alongside leadership skills. For example, you may be on the management team of a finance department or a partner in a legal practice. If so, then whenever I refer to a leadership framework below you will want to add appropriate areas of technical expertise too.

Assuming that you want to identify those with leadership potential, you and your colleagues need to articulate the leadership attributes that indicate this. Your discussions of talent will be based on your framework of leadership attributes (Figure 8.2).

Stage two: who are your talented people?

Having established the qualities you are looking for, the next stage is to review your people and make some collective decisions on who seems most likely to be successful as a future leader. A good place to start is with effective one-to-one development reviews between individuals and their line manager. This provides essential information – on strengths, weaknesses, aspirations and development needs – for you and your colleagues to meet together in a *talent review* which discusses people and agrees who seems most talented.

These two steps – individual development reviews and a management team's talent review – may be enough to identify

Figure 8.3 Who are your talented people?

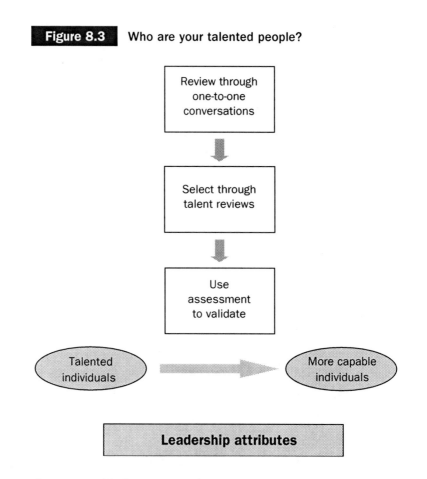

those most likely to succeed. However, you may want to use some additional assessment to verify or amend your selections, perhaps by running some form of assessment centre or by involving someone such as an occupational psychologist to interview and test your people (Figure 8.3).

Stage three: how will you develop this talent?

These first two stages have enabled you and your colleagues to identify with some robustness and confidence the people you think are most likely to succeed in future leadership roles. I want to emphasise that you are still only at first base. The real challenge is to do things that will build the capability of your talented people. The most valuable action you can take in most cases is to offer your talented people new experiences that will challenge and stretch them. As Morgan McCall says in *High Flyers*, 'The principle is simple: most people learn most by doing things they haven't done before'.

As well as offering people fresh experiences, you also have to help them to reflect on and learn from these opportunities. To do this, you simply need to use those processes such as coaching, mentoring and feedback that we covered in previous chapters.

You might also want to give your talented people the opportunity to take part in a significant development programme, such as a spell at business school or the chance to take part in your organisation's flagship leadership programme, if you have one.

To sum up (Figure 8.4), your prime objective in talent management is to identify talented individuals and help them to become more capable. To do this effectively you need the following:

- a general framework of what you are looking for in individuals;

- a means of deciding – against this framework – which individuals are most talented;

- ways of developing the capability of these talented people.

The remainder of the chapter looks in more detail at the key elements of stages one, two and three in turn.

Figure 8.4 How will you develop this talent?

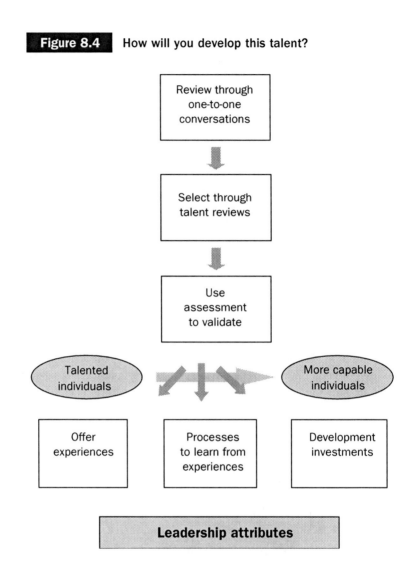

A model of leadership qualities and behaviours

When you and your colleagues on a management team meet to discuss talent, you will find it very helpful to have clear criteria to define what you are looking for. This gives you a language to use in the conversation. Where clear criteria have not been articulated, there is a real danger that your discussion will be unfocused, based on anecdote, highly subjective and perhaps dominated by the comments of one or two people.

A framework of leadership attributes – that is, the qualities the organisation is looking for in its future leaders – helps to focus the discussion around the table on specific attitudes and behaviours demonstrated by each individual being reviewed. The discussion will still be subjective, but based on judgments of individual qualities backed up by supporting evidence.

In this chapter I am assuming that you are looking to develop the future leaders of your organisation rather than those who will play key roles in specific disciplines. If you are looking to develop talent in a technical area, such as finance or HR, you will need to add technical capability to your leadership attributes.

While it is possible to take a generic leadership framework that has been created by someone else, there is enormous benefit in you and your colleagues articulating with clarity the attributes you are looking for in future leaders. First, this grounds the leadership framework in the reality of your organisation and its strategy. Note that it is more useful to articulate the qualities that will be needed for the future success of your organisation rather than necessarily on what made it successful in the past. Second, your management team will have more ownership of – and indeed understanding of – the framework if you created it. Third, you can deploy the leadership framework in a variety of other ways within the organisation – in performance reviews, in selection interviews, and as the basis of a

360-degree feedback process, for example – and it will be taken more seriously if it was shaped by the management team.

One way of creating the framework – which is best done ahead of any talent review meeting – is for a facilitator to interview you and your management colleagues, to pull together your views into a draft framework, and to help your management team agree the final version and form of words.

Table 8.1 illustrates what a set of leadership attributes might look like, set out on one sheet of paper. Note that I am not advocating that you simply lift this framework – as I say, there will be more understanding and commitment if the framework has been created within your organisation.

Table 8.1 A set of leadership attributes

Vision	Articulating future possibilities that will transform the current situation.
Drive	Having the will, ambition, energy and resilience to stand out from the crowd and proactively make things happen.
Personal presence	Demonstrating the self confidence, gravitas and ability to speak convincingly that influences people and events.
Integrity	Acting consistently with a clear set of personal values that includes dealing with others fairly and honestly.
Judgment	Using a blend of common sense, intuition, wisdom and analytical skills to make high quality decisions.
Emotional intelligence	Having a high awareness of the feelings of self and others, together with the self control and social skills to interact effectively with most people.

Effective one-to-one development reviews

A development review is a discussion between you and an individual who works for you which considers their strengths, weaknesses, aspirations and development needs, leading to the creation of a personal development plan.

The quality of a development review will be higher when:

- your relationship has a degree of openness, and the discussion is based on adult-to-adult conversation;
- they genuinely want to build their capability and are prepared to take responsibility for their own learning and development;
- you are keen to support them in building their capability and making a greater contribution to the organisation;
- both of you take responsibility for making the review meaningful;
- both of you respect differences in your values and ways of working.

Chapter 2 showed an example of a development review form built around half a dozen coaching questions focused on the individual:

- What are your strengths, both job related and behavioural?
- What are your weaknesses, both job related and behavioural?
- What are your aspirations – in the short, medium and long term? What are you prepared to do to achieve these?

- What new experiences or challenges would you like over the next twelve months? What support do you need from your manager?

- In what areas do you want to develop your capability over the next twelve months? In each area, what will you do – and by when – to develop yourself?

Development reviews which explore these questions provide essential input to a talent discussion. It will enable you to speak in a more informed and structured way about your people to your colleagues.

A talent review meeting

When you and your colleagues come together for a talent review meeting, you are seeking to do two things:

- reach a shared view of the capability and potential of your people;

- agree developmental actions that will release this potential.

Talent review meetings can be held at different levels in an organisation. One way of ensuring that discussions take place at the most appropriate level is through an *upward cascade* of talent reviews. Successively higher levels of management team meet to review those below them. The process culminates in a talent review involving the top team. In some organisations this might be the only talent review, while in others there might be several levels of review in the upward cascade.

The following procedure is a useful way of structuring a talent review meeting. It is generally very helpful to have someone in the role of facilitator cum secretary who can keep the meeting on track and who can record agreements and actions. This also frees the leader of the management team to take full part in the debate on individuals, and generally their views will be extremely influential.

- Circulate in advance the names of those who will be discussed. If this is not done in advance, it is useful to record on a flipchart at the opening of the meeting who will be discussed.

- Discuss each individual for around 15 minutes. The discussion begins with the presenting manager (who will normally be the line manager of the individual) summarising their view of the individual's strengths, weaknesses, aspirations and development plans. This information will normally have been gathered during a one-to-one development review with that individual. It is also useful to share brief details of the individual's career background, current role and professional qualifications.

- Other members of the group add their views of the individual. It is important that this discussion is an open and honest sharing of opinions about the individual, based on observed behaviour rather than superficial impressions, hearsay or prejudice. This sharing of views creates a wider understanding among the management team of the individual's capability and potential. As noted above, an agreed framework of leadership attributes helps to focus this discussion.

- In many talent reviews the discussion is summarised in a conclusion or in some kind of rating. As an illustration, some talent reviews categorise people's readiness to move to the next level in the organisation as:

  - ready now;
  - ready within two years;
  - not ready within two years.

It is not essential to summarise in this kind of way, and it might even be unhelpful. While a summary offers the reassurance of a clear conclusion to the discussion, it may also be an oversimplification of how someone is regarded.

- Consider and agree actions to enhance the development of the individual. Note that the individual needs genuinely to buy into a development plan if the actions are to make a real difference to their development,

- Move on to the next individual on the list.

The talent review form shown in Figure 8.5 conveniently builds on the individual development review form from

Figure 8.5　A talent review form

TALENT REVIEW

Individual being reviewed　　　　　*Date of meeting*
Presenting manager　　　　　*Facilitator/secretary*
Chair of meeting

STRENGTHS:

WEAKNESSES:

ASPIRATIONS: *(as seen by the individual)*

POTENTIAL: *(Is the reviewee ready to move to a higher level now, or within two years?)*

FRESH EXPERIENCE? *(Such as job move, secondment, project work, non exec role, deputising opportunity. Who will be responsible for making this happen, and by when?)*

OTHER ACTIONS? *(Such as external coaching, internal mentoring, 360-degree feedback or nomination to development workshop or programme. Who will be responsible for making this happen, and by when?)*

Note: The presenting manager should check the contents of this form and then review these as part of a feedback conversation with the individual. Once reviewed, the contents will also be entered into the talent management database

---

Chapter 2, and is useful for presenting and summarising views of an individual and for recording agreed actions. This can also be the basis for providing feedback to the individual and for updating a talent database if you have one.

It is also vital that as a management team you review these actions, say, three months later to check progress and ensure that good intentions are being translated into reality. The aggregate of the actions from the meeting can be regarded as a 90-day plan. If you are holding talent reviews once a year, you may find that a 12-month gap is too long to monitor progress in implementing actions.

Feedback after a talent review

One outcome of a talent review meeting is that you and your colleagues will be better informed about the talent within your organisation. Another outcome is that, having listened to how your colleagues see some of your key people, you will have valuable feedback to share. Unfortunately, not all managers share this feedback with their people.

In my view, sharing feedback with each of your people after a talent review is important if the organisation wants to create a culture of open, adult to adult relationships. There will sometimes be views that need editing or censoring, but in a mature organisation each individual discussed will receive feedback on how the management team see their strengths, weaknesses and potential. This feedback conversation also gives the opportunity to win the individual's commitment to development actions – or to modify proposed actions in discussion with the individual.

The degree to which this kind of conversation takes place will reflect the wider culture of the organisation, itself largely a product of the behaviours which the top team role model. Cultures take time to shift, but one way for a management team to signal a change to a more open culture would be to make the talent review process more transparent.

In many organisations the talent review process is treated as confidential and even those on the high potential list are not told how they are regarded. In a more open process, those who are seen as having the potential to go further are told. Most people will be pleased to hear this, and will feel motivated to continue performing well. Occasionally, someone might indicate that they are not so career-oriented and would rather not be offered challenging opportunities. It is best that this is made explicit because otherwise you may be investing scarce development opportunities in someone who does not want them.

For those who do not feature on the high potential list, you again need to consider what you will share with them. In an open process, you will tell each of the people reviewed how they are regarded by the management team. Someone who is told that they are not seen as having the potential to go further has three basic choices – to prove through their performance that the management team need to revise their view, to accept that their career has reached a plateau, or to leave the organisation and fulfil their potential elsewhere.

Information from talent reviews is generally recorded in some form, whether in a formal database or merely as meeting notes. In either case, an individual may ask to see what is recorded against their name. Where the talent review process is open and feedback given to each individual, then Data Protection Act (1984) problems can be avoided.

Information on people

In a talent review a management team will be putting forward and listening to views on people. As we noted earlier, it is very helpful to have a framework of, say, leadership attributes to focus this conversation. This framework provides a shared language for discussing people and their attributes. You and your colleagues are more likely to understand this language if your views created it in the first place.

The model of information in Figure 8.6 offers one perspective on the challenge facing a group in discussing people. It is based on the ideas set out by Max Boisot in his book *Information and Organization.*

Information may be more or less easily codified and information may be more or less widely disseminated. The emergency telephone number, 999, is an example of a piece of information that is very clearly codified and is widely disseminated. The Personal Identification Number of your bank cash card is highly codified but is only known to you and certain bank employees. It is not widely disseminated, and this is entirely appropriate.

Figure 8.6   A model of information (after Max Boisot)

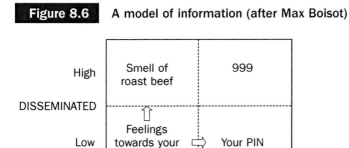

The smell of roast beef, on the other hand, is information that most of us know – it is widely disseminated. However, it is not well codified. We would struggle to put into words or numbers what roast beef smells like.

You may not have thought about your first boss for many years, and may never have identified exactly what you felt about them. And perhaps no one else knows your feelings towards your first boss. Your feelings about them is information which is neither highly codified nor highly disseminated.

The skill of a wine expert lies in their ability to recognise and communicate the tastes and smells of individual wines. That is, they can to some extent codify and disseminate information that is somewhat difficult to codify and disseminate.

One way of looking at the challenge facing your management team in a talent review meeting, therefore, is that you are using information on people which is neither well codified (because it is subjective, impressionistic, anecdotal) nor disseminated among you (if you are not used to reviewing your talented people). You need to codify this more effectively – and the use of a leadership framework helps to do this – and you need to disseminate it more effectively, by regularly having high-quality conversations where you meet to review talent.

It is an oversimplification to reduce the talents of an individual to a single number, such as 999. However, some talent review processes in fact do this – for example, by agreeing ratings for an individual on each of the leadership attributes and then totalling these. Moreover, a talent review process that concludes with a list of, say, those ready for promotion now, those ready within two years and those who won't be ready within two years are in effect using a three-point scale to summarise and codify collective views on people. If your succession review process does reduce the discussion of individuals to a single rating, I encourage you to make sure your regularly revisit these assessments to see if any of them are out-of-date.

An independent assessment process

The process described so far will have established those whom you and your management colleagues regard as talented when considered against your framework of leadership attributes. While it is possible at this stage to move into agreeing development actions, you may want to consider building in some kind of independent process to verify and perhaps amend the assessments made on individuals. The decisions made on people and the movement of people into key roles are important both for the individuals and the organisation, and it is worth spending time getting these right.

One way to carry out assessments of capability and potential is to run an assessment centre. A number of individuals are brought together to complete a series of tasks and possibly psychometric tests, with others observing them and later reviewing what they noticed. This is a time-consuming and expensive process, but it may offer a more informed view of individuals and – particularly if senior managers are involved as assessors – can have great face validity within the organisation.

One caution about assessment centres is that they can sometimes identify those who come across well at assessment centres rather than those are truly the most capable. For example, extraverts will tend to create a more favourable impression than introverts. A well-designed assessment centre will take this into account.

Another way to validate assessments of individuals is to utilise someone such as an occupational psychologist to take each individual through a range of psychometric and aptitude tests, an interview covering career history and perhaps behavioural competencies, and possibly to listen to a presentation by the individual. The occupational psychologist then produces a report on strengths, weaknesses, development priorities and assessment of potential. This may or may not be shared with the individual, and sometimes two reports are produced – one for the individual and another, usually more hard-hitting, for the organisation.

A downside to the use of a consultant – either external or internal – to carry out the assessment is that the results are less likely to be owned and to be fully understood than when senior managers are involved through an assessment centre. Senior managers observing an individual may form some views that they cannot fully articulate or that they choose to keep to themselves, and this is still relevant intelligence. On the other hand, a consultant who is an experienced assessor is less likely to bring personal biases to the assessment than some senior managers.

360-degree or other feedback from people who know the individual can also be woven into an assessment centre or one-to-one assessments. This enriches the process by incorporating wider views of the individual which capture how they operate from day to day and under pressure in the real world outside an assessment process.

There is one other process I have heard of which combines the best of a group discussion about an individual with the importance of having people in the conversation who know from first-hand how that individual operates from day to day. This process brings together those who have managed the individual over their last three or four roles. One possible practical difficulty, particularly in a fast-moving industry sector, may be that these line managers are no longer in the organisation.

Opportunities to gain new experiences

The talent review process described up to this point has robustly identified and confirmed the names of those regarded within your organisation as its most talented people. This, however, is merely to get to first base in talent management. Something needs to happen beyond that. Talent reviews must also lead to action – job moves or other significant developmental investments – for the process to be alive, meaningful and adding value to your organisation.

The most valuable development experiences in the workplace usually come from tackling a new job. If your organisation is serious about proactively nurturing its talented people you need to be regularly moving key people into new roles. As Morgan McCall says, 'Because such a large number of the experiences important to the development of executive leadership skills occur through work assignments, the critical question is clearly, "Who gets what job?"'.

The seriousness with which talent reviews are taken in your organisation will depend crucially on the stance of the person at the top. Moving people requires both commitment and finesse, and will only happen effectively when the chief executive (or equivalent) really wants it to happen. The final section of this chapter looks further at how vital it is to have the active support of the person at the top.

The chief executive will also, however, require commitment from their colleagues. For movement to occur, senior people have to be willing both to let their talented people move into other parts of the organisation and to take new people into their department. They are more likely to release talented people when taking this wider corporate perspective is genuinely recognised as important in the organisation and is valued by the chief executive.

In placing a talented manager in a challenging role where they will learn new things, the organisation has to balance the development of that manager with the need for an effective performer who will deliver what the organisation requires. This is inevitably a matter of judgment – a trade-off between investing in development to yield future performance against short-term delivery of results.

There is also a logistical issue in timing and phasing job moves so that as one person leaves a role, someone else takes over without undue delay. An organisation might have an annual 'transfer season' during which succession moves typically take place in a coordinated way. Some organisations have roles which are regarded as development positions and which are filled, for example, for two years by a talented person rising through the company. It is easier to move talent into new jobs when an organisation is expanding and needs to create new or bigger roles. In a more static environment, it may be essential to identify who needs to move out of the way to let talent come through. Ideally, the organisation will be managing this proactively and providing attractive incentives to those who have served loyally and who are no longer needed. Conversations about individuals whom you want to step aside – and feedback to these individuals – may be part of the overall talent management process.

While a new and challenging job provides the richest vehicle for development, there are other ways of giving people opportunities to build their capability. A secondment to a new role or the chance to lead a major project will provide real-time experiences for development. Non-executive opportunities can also be extremely valuable. These may be within the organisation – for example sitting as a non-exec on the board or management team of a subsidiary company – or in another organisation. Offering someone a non-exec position indicates a powerful commitment to the individual, which in turn can aid motivation and retention of that person.

Finding non-executive opportunities

There are a number of places where you might look to find a developmental non-exec opportunity for your talented people. These provide a 'win-win' situation where the receiving organisation benefits from the experience and knowledge of the talented manager while they in turn learn new things through having to take a strategic view and by looking at the world from the different perspective of another organisation.

Hanson Green, who describe themselves as the UK's leader in the field of non-exec appointments, run an ANNEX scheme. This is designed to provide developmental opportunities for talented managers to take a non-exec role in an organisation such as a dot.com start-up or a management buy-out. There is a five-figure fee for placing someone via the ANNEX scheme, but the cost can be more than recouped by having the director's fee paid to the organisation rather than the individual. Candidates spend three years as a non-exec director, and are expected to be available for a maximum of 15 days a year. This sounds like an excellent way of developing someone who ultimately will become a director within their own organisation.

Arts & Business is a charity which specialises in bringing together people from these two different fields. Under their Board Bank scheme, someone from the business world brings their experience and expertise to the Board of an arts organisation. The fresh and exciting surroundings of the arts world can be very stimulating and enjoyable for someone whose full-time role is in business.

Public appointments offer the opportunity to make a contribution to public life, to gain an insight into the process of government, to network, and to develop skills. Interchange is a government initiative to encourage the exchange of people and ideas between the Civil Service and other areas of the economy. Every government department has an Interchange programme. A variety of opportunities are possible, including secondments lasting between three months and three years. There are also opportunities to work as a non-exec or an advisor to boards, committees or project teams.

The Whitehall & Industry Group has a scheme to facilitate the placing of managers from industry as non-exec directors on Whitehall management boards, and of high-flying civil servants in industry. They also broker short attachments and long-term secondments in both directions.

The Public Appointments Unit in the Cabinet Office maintains a register of 6,000 names of individuals who are willing to be considered for a wide range of roles in public office. The Unit itself does not make appointments, but makes names known to the relevant Departments. Some of these bodies are of national importance with budgets in excess of a billion pounds. Individuals may put their own name forward to the Public Appointments Unit.

Processes to learn from these experiences

Having set up an opportunity for a talented individual to take part in a challenging experience, it is also important that you ensure that they have the chance to reflect on and make sense of their experience if they are to learn and build their capability. In earlier chapters we looked at the use of coaching, mentoring and feedback as ways of helping people both to learn through reflection and also to enhance their performance. An effective talent review process will put in place mechanisms such as these explicitly to encourage learning and development.

Some form of coaching or mentoring support can be particularly useful during the first 100 days in a new position to help the individual to clarify their role, identify the main stakeholders, decide on their own key deliverables, and work out how they will use their time. A talented individual may well set up their own support mechanisms, particularly if the organisation does not do so. Similarly, an explicit review at the end of an assignment – individually or in conversation with a coach or line manager – can articulate and enhance the learning and set up development goals for the next challenging opportunity.

In contrast, some organisations in effect test their talented people to destruction. They offer talented people bigger and bigger roles until eventually they fail to deliver. Instead of an honest review of what went wrong and what can be learnt for next time – both by the individual and by the organisation which may have made a mistake in placing them in this role – the failed manager is at best derailed from the fast track or at worst dismissed.

Key development investments

We have seen that offering talented people new challenges is the prime way of building their capability and releasing their potential. Sometimes, however, a talent review will decide that the most useful experience for an individual is to stay in their current role for, say, another year or 18 months.

Talent reviews are also an appropriate forum for deciding on other significant investments in the development of individuals. For example, an organisation may have a flagship leadership development programme, and participation in this is seen as an excellent way of learning and networking, as a badge of recognition, and sometimes as an essential pre-requisite for senior roles.

Another major investment in the development of an individual is to take part in a significant programme at a business school. Most leading business schools offer four- or six-week programmes – sometimes longer – where talented managers can learn about themselves and what they stand for, about leadership and about areas such as strategy, finance and marketing. On top of this, a spell at business school offers an opportunity to network with leaders from other organisations, which most people find extremely useful both at the time and into the future. The largest investment here is for the organisation to fund the individual to take an MBA. This may be on either part-time basis – where the individual continues work in the organisation – or on a full-time basis, typically for a year or so.

Note that one downside to developing talented people – particularly if this involves collecting a marketable badge such as an MBA from a prestigious business school – is that the individual becomes more attractive to other companies.

A further possibility is through short programmes run by organisations such as the Windsor Leadership Trust, the Centre for Management and Policy Studies within the Cabinet Office, or the Whitehall & Industry Group. These enable talented managers to mix with their counterparts from different walks of life – business, public sector, charities, church, armed forces, and so on. These again provide a chance for a talented manager to compare themselves with others, to build a network, to see the world from very different perspectives, and to learn about leadership.

A talent management database

If your organisation is spending time reviewing talent and agreeing job moves and other development actions, it is important to capture information and decisions in an appropriate format.

One of the world's leading IT companies, a multinational company whose name is a household word across the globe, spent many years and millions of dollars trying to create databases to store and retrieve intelligence on people. They concluded that their efforts had been wasted, and that local databases were the most useful. Local in this case did not necessarily mean geographically local but rather focused on a particular population (for example, the finance community).

At the other end of the scale there are organisations where the talent database sits inside the head of the chief executive or possibly in a little black book that they keep.

Having been involved in a number of attempts to establish databases of intelligence on people, I have reached a similar conclusion to the IT company. My advice on creating a talent management database is to be ruthlessly clear about the key purposes of the database, to limit who has access to it (not because of secrecy but to minimise the complexity of your software), and to resist ideas to take the scope beyond issues regarding talent. It might be essential for the chief executive to have every senior manager's home phone number easily accessible, but this is not part of the talent management database. It is also important that you record the actions agreed at talent reviews.

I do not think that you actually have to computerise the database. A secure filing cabinet with paper copies of talent review forms, performance records, CVs and basic biographical data will suffice. However, it is efficient to computerise this in a fit-for-purpose database that stores what you want and lets you print information on each individual in a well laid out format that can be presented to the management team.

I am sceptical about databases which let you search under various criteria to identify, for example, engineers with an MBA who speak fluent Spanish. This information can be found in a search because it is easily codified. In reality, the criteria that matter will include less easily codified factors such as skill in negotiations, capability in project management and extent of overseas experience. All of these, including the last, require judgments (six months of one kind of overseas experience might be more useful than six years of another), and these judgments are probably being made by different people with different standards.

The talent review form shown in Figure 8.5 – along with basic CV data – provides the key information you need to set up a fit-for-purpose talent management database. Remember that one advantage of a more open process is that you can avoid complications with the Data Protection Act (1984).

A critical roles model of succession management

Some organisations use a succession management process based on first identifying the critical roles within the organisation and then deciding who is ready now or in, say, two years' time to fill these roles. The approach provides some reassurance that the organisation has plans to replace key people if they depart for whatever reason. I have some reservations about this approach, however.

First, the process may be identifying those needed to run today's organisation rather than tomorrow's. We live in a rapidly changing world, where technology, markets, competition and regulation continually pose new challenges. Moreover, organisations are forming and reforming through acquisition or disposal, merger or demerger. Thus the critical roles identified today may not even exist at the end of the year.

Second, the critical roles approach can get into a circular argument about what the critical roles are. The critical roles may be regarded as those filled with the key people, while the key people are those filling the critical roles. One way to avoid this circularity is simply to define all senior roles as critical and identify successors for all of them.

The *pools of talent* approach set out in this chapter avoids the circularity and possible inflexibility of the *critical roles* approach. Nevertheless, in an organisation which has a degree of stability and where the majority of tomorrow's senior roles are likely to exist today, a critical roles model of succession management provides a practical starting point for discussing future leaders and their development.

The commitment of the chief executive

Actions speak louder than words. Any chief executive has to deal with a myriad of issues demanding their time and attention. The things that your chief executive spends time on send messages to senior managers and shape the culture of the organisation. The unfortunate reality in many organisations is that learning and development issues get displaced by other concerns.

However, unless the chief executive is genuinely committed to making talent management effective, then it is impossible to make it really work. Equally, when the chief executive demonstrates real commitment through their actions, then talent management comes alive.

An illustration of a chief executive who took leadership development seriously is Larry Bossidy. As CEO of the US firm AlliedSignal, Bossidy transformed the fortunes of the company. He reckons that he spent between 30–40% of his time in the first two years hiring and developing leaders. He writes in the *Harvard Business Review* that he is 'convinced that AlliedSignal's success was due in large part to the amount of time and emotional commitment [he] devoted to leadership development'. He concludes that:

> Many executives have neglected a personal involvement, accountability, and initiative in developing leaders within their organisations. But because it is full of unknowns, of unpredictability, it deserves more time than anything else you do as CEO. (Bossidy, 2001)

Or, in the words of Morgan McCall, 'Above all, the development of leadership is a leadership issue'.

Bibliography

Boisot, M. (1987) *Information and Organization*. London: Fontana.

Bossidy, L. (2001) 'The Job No CEO Should Delegate'. *Harvard Business Review*, 79 (3), pp. 46–49, 163.

Boud, D., Keogh, R. and Walker, D. (1985) *Reflection: Turning Experience into Learning*. London: Kogan Page.

Chapman, M. (2001) *The Emotional Intelligence Pocketbook*. Alresford: Management Pocketbooks.

Critchley, W. and Casey, D. (1984) 'Second Thoughts on Team Building'. *Management Education and Development*, 15 (2), pp. 163–175.

Downey, M. (2003) *Effective Coaching*. London: Texere.

Flick, D. (1998) *From Debate to Dialogue*. Boulder: Orchid.

Fraser, D. (1993) *Knight's Cross*. London: HarperCollins.

Gallwey, T. (2000) *The Inner Game of Work*. New York: Random House.

Goleman, D. (1996) *Emotional Intelligence*. London: Bloomsbury.

Harris, T. (1974) *I'm OK – You're OK*. Boston: G K Hall.

Harvey Jones, J. (1988) *Making It Happen*. London: Collins.

Honey, P. and Mumford, A. (2000) *The Learning Styles Helper's Guide*. Maidenhead: Peter Honey Publications.

Isaacs, W. (1999) *Dialogue and the Art of Thinking Together*. New York: Currency Doubleday.

Katzenbach, J. and Smith, D. (1994) *The Wisdom of Teams*. New York: Harper.

Knowles, M. (1984) *The Adult Learner: A Neglected Species*. Houston: Gulf.

Kolb, D. (1984) *Experiential Learning*. Englewood Cliffs: Prentice-Hall.

Kotter J. (1982) *The General Managers*. New York: Free Press.

McCall, M. (1998) *High Flyers*. Boston: Harvard Business School.

Mintzberg, H. (2004) *Managers Not MBAs*. San Francisco: Berrett-Koehler.

Morgan, G. (1996) *Images of Organization*. Thousand Oaks: Sage.

Pedler, M. (1996) *Action Learning for Managers*. Lemos and Crane, London.

Rogers, C. (1961) *On Becoming a Person*. Boston: Houghton Mifflin.

Scott, S. (2002) *Fierce Conversations*. London: Piatkus.

Senge, P. (1990) *The Fifth Discipline*. New York: Currency Doubleday.

Stone, D., Patton, B. and Heen, S. (1999) *Difficult Conversations*. New York: Viking Penguin.

Taylor, M. (1979) *Coverdale on Management*. London: Heinemann.

van Eupen, P. and Rajan A. (1996) *Leading People*. Tunbridge Wells: Centre for Research and Technology in Europe.

Wheatley, M. (2002) *Turning to One Another*. San Francisco: Berrett-Koehler.

Whitaker D. (1999) *The Spirit of Teams*. Marlborough: Crowood.

Whitmore, J. (2002) *Coaching for Performance*. London: Nicholas Brealey.

Index

action learning, 68–69
adult:adult relationships, 93–96, 127,
   131–132
AlliedSignal, 146
ANNEX scheme, 139
Argyris, Chris, 106
Aristotle, 97
Arts and Business, 139–140
assessment centres, 122, 135–136
awareness, 22, 44–45, 68, 72

Blanchard, Ken, 41
Boisot, Max, 133
Bossidy, Larry, 146
Boud, David, 7
Buber, Martin, 87
Bush, George W, 88

Cabinet Office, 140, 142
Casey, David, 75
Centre for Management and Policy
   Studies, 142
Change Partnership, The, 22
Chapman, Margaret, 97–98
Clutterbuck, David, 55, 57, 62
coaching, 19–39, 41, 44, 55–56, 59,
   63, 95, 123, 127, 128, 141
  and development reviews, 38–39
  and 360-degree feedback, 52–53
  as a relationship, 23–25
  dance, 36–38
  executive, 66–67
  silent, 32–35
  teams, 71–74
command and control, 20, 23–26, 60,
   91–92
confidentiality, 35–36, 60, 132
conversations, 46–47, 96, 101–118,
   131, 138

difficult, 113–116
  learning, 115–116
Coverdale, Ralph, 83
Coverdale Systematic Approach,
   83–86
CPS, 56
Critchley, Bill, 75
cycle:
  of control, 25–26
  of development, 26–28
  of empowerment, 26–27
  see also learning cycle

Data Protection Act, 132, 144
debate, 101–103, 105, 111–112, 115
definitions:
  coaching, 22
  learning, 4
  learning organisation, 80–81
  mentoring, 56
  team, 74–75
development reviews, 38–39,
   121–122, 127–128, 130
dialogue, 101–103, 105, 108, 110,
   111–112, 115
directive and non-directive coaching,
   23
Downey, Myles, 72

Einstein, Albert, 5
emotional intelligence, 96–100
emotions, 29, 43–44, 99, 100,
   103–104, 112, 113–114
empowerment, 25–28

feedback, 37, 41–53, 123, 131–132,
   136, 138, 141
  after a talent review, 131–132
  for teams, 73

five levels of, 45–46
gathering, 48–50
generating, 44–47
giving and receiving, 42–44
360-degree, 50–53, 136
feedforward, 47–48
feelings, *see* emotions
Flick, Deborah, 111
Four player system, 117–118
Fraser, David, 11–12

Galileo, 13
Gallwey, Tim, 13
Goleman, Daniel, 96, 98
Greenleaf, Robert, 92
GROW framework:
for coaching, 31–35
with teams, 72–73

Hanson Green, 139
Hardingham, Alison, 88, 115
Harris, Thomas, 93–94
Harvey Jones, John, 86
Hayden, Gina, 103, 109, 111
Heen, Sheila, *see* Stone, Douglas
Hemery, David, 36–37
Henshaw, George, 110
Hirst, Deana, 62
Honda, 81
Honey, Peter, 10, 80
Huxley, Aldous, 6

iceberg diagram, 104
ICI, 86
information:
model, 133–134
on people, 133–135, 143–144
inquiring, 104–106, 112
Interchange, 140
Isaacs, Bill, 103, 117

journalling, 7–9, 99

Kantor, David, 116–118
Katzenbach, Jon, 74, 75
Keogh, Rosemary, 7
Kipling, Rudyard, 30
Knowing, 4–6
Kolb, David, 1–7, 10, 80
Kotter, John, 27–28

ladder of inference, 106–107
language, three languages of
communicating, 116–117
Lao Tse, 71
Large, Will, 62
leadership model, a, 121, 123,
124–126
learning cycle, 2–4, 9–10
learning from experience, 1–17,
37, 39, 41, 57, 123,
140–141
for teams, 74, 81
learning organisation, 16, 80–86
learning styles, 10–12
Lewin, Kurt, 1, 4
listening, 22, 28–29, 34, 36, 45,
59, 60, 68, 100, 103–104,
109–110, 112

management by objectives, 20, 91
manager coach, 35–38, 95
managing people:
coaching approach, 21–23
conventional approach, 19–21
MBA, 142
see also Mintzberg, Henry
McCall, Morgan, 13, 16, 17, 25, 119,
123, 137, 146
McGill, Madeline, 8
mentoring, 55–69, 123, 141
guidelines for a mentoring scheme,
62–65
peer mentoring, 67–68
metaphors, 80–81
of manager, 91–93
of organisations, 88–91
Mintzberg, Henry, 7, 15
Morgan, Gareth, 89–91
Mumford, Alan, 10

non-directive, 23, 57, 59, 60
non-executive opportunities,
139–140

off-job courses, 14–15
organisational memory, 81–83

Patton, Bruce, *see* Stone, Douglas
Pedler, Mike, 68
Public Appointments Unit, 140

questioning, 22, 28, 29–31, 34–35,
     36, 45, 59, 68
  and feedforward, 47–48
  and 360 degree feedback, 52–53
  open questions, 30–31, 33–34,
     38–39, 45–46, 47–48, 52–53
  to generate feedback, 45–46
  see also inquiring

Rajan, Amin, 56
relationships, 87–100, 101–102,
     103–104, 108, 127
  and feedback, 46–47
  and listening, 28, 103–104
  and mentoring, 56, 60, 61–62
  coaching as relationship, 23–25

responsibility, 22, 26–27, 45, 69, 72
Rogers, Carl, 1, 13
role analysis, 48–50
Rommel, Erwin, 11–12

Scott, Susan, 19, 43, 104, 111, 113
self talk, 44, 99
Senge, Peter, 2, 16, 80, 92, 106
servant leadership, 92
Shakespeare, William, 4
silence, 29, 110–111
Smith, Douglas, 74, 75
strategy for developing people,
     12–14
Stone, Douglas, 108, 113, 115, 116
succession management:
  critical roles model, 144–145
  see also talent management

Summerfield, Jenny, 42–43, 44
systematic approach, 83–86

talent management, 119–146
  database, 143–144
  mentor as sponsor, 65–66
talent reviews, 121–123, 128–131,
     134, 142
Taylor, Max, 85
teams, 71–79
  coaching, 71–74
  definition, 74–76
  development exercise, 78–79
  stages of development, 76–77
telling, 20–21, 23, 36–37, 47
thinking rounds, 109–110
top management, commitment of,
     137, 145–146
  environment created by, 16–17
transactional analysis, 93–96

validated listening, 110
van Eupen, Penny, 56
voicing, 107–109, 112

Walker, David, 7
Wheatley, Meg, 24, 96, 103–104,
     105–106, 113
Whitaker, David, 76
Whitehall & Industry Group, 140,
     142
Whitmore, John, 22, 23, 31, 45–46,
     47, 76
Whyte, David, 101
Windsor Leadership Trust, 142

Printed in the United Kingdom
by Lightning Source UK Ltd.
123084UK00001B/181/A

9 781843 342137